Message from the Director

Connie L. Patrick
Director
Federal Law Enforcement Training Center
U.S. Department of Homeland Security
1131 Chapel Crossing Road
Glynco, Georgia 31524

   In support of our ongoing mission to provide world-class training, the Federal Law Enforcement Training Center (FLETC) is pleased to present this report on *Stress and Decision Making*. FLETC's Training Research Branch has expanded upon its original research in the area of stress and decision making to identify new strategies that enhance law enforcement training. This booklet contains four sections that identify: training strategies to improve officer decision making under stress, an improved process for providing feedback to trainees, a more accurate and consistent measure for scoring scenario performance, and an analysis of trainee performance in lethal and non-lethal confrontations.

   The FLETC is pleased to share this information with the law enforcement community and contribute to the growing body of knowledge in this area. I would like to thank our partner organizations at the FLETC for providing their support and the students that made this research possible. The FLETC remains dedicated to exploring new methodologies in the pursuit of providing the best training possible to the law enforcement organizations we serve. *Stress and Decision Making* is one of the ways the FLETC uses applied research to determine the most effective training strategies that prepare law enforcement officers to meet their ever-evolving responsibilities.

Connie L. Patrick

Connie L. Patrick
Director
Federal Law Enforcement Training Center

Research Overview

In 2000, the Federal Law Enforcement Training Center initiated a research project that recorded and reviewed the tactical responses of trainees who faced a novel scenario that rapidly transitioned from routine report writing to actions requiring the use of deadly force. A second phase of the research was conducted to build on the initial findings and explore further the multiple aspects of performance under stress. This paper, *Stress and Decision Making*, provides the results and training implications from the second phase. It is our hope that these findings will be applied to multiple training areas including scenario realism, physiological and psychological responses to stress, consistent and accurate scenario scoring, building mental models to improve decision making under stress, and identifying an effective process for delivering feedback to students that will in turn reduce errors and improve future performance.

In order to rate performance consistently between multiple evaluators and across both lethal and non-lethal scenarios, a new rating system, Scenario Training Assessment and Review (STAR) was created. STAR consists of eight areas of acceptable student performance—survival factors—which reflect the student's ability to make decisions under threat conditions, then implement those decisions to control the situation. In addition, a new scoring system (risk-based assessment scale) was developed to objectively determine acceptable performance.

One of the eight STAR factors, *Articulation/After Action Review (AAR)*, focuses on the student providing factual and accurate information during the debriefing session. Although this factor is the final component of the STAR, it provides meaningful information and the insight needed for another new training tool evaluated during the study—Student-Centered Feedback. The subjects in the study demonstrated that feedback that is student-centered can be more meaningful and provides greater benefit than traditional types of after action reviews. These findings suggest that the STAR assessment model, combined with Student-Centered Feedback using video supplementation, are ideal tools to enhance training effectiveness and establish accurate mental models (memories)—essential for effective law enforcement responses in dynamic, high stress confrontations such as those presented in this study.

William A. Norris, Ph.D.
Chief
Training Research Branch
Training Innovation Division

Terry N. Wollert, Ph.D.
Senior Researcher
Training Research Branch
Training Innovation Division

Preface

It has been a great privilege to have had the opportunity to work on the Survival Scores Research Project with colleagues and staff at the Federal Law Enforcement Training Center. FLETC leadership is to be congratulated in having had the vision to initiate research assessing performance under realistically stressful conditions, with a view to evaluating the training program.

While entrusted with the protection of some of the most vulnerable members of society, law enforcement officers must be prepared also to deal with extremely dangerous situations and individuals. Accurate assessments and judgments must be made and correct actions taken in fractions of a second. A wrong or late decision can have tragic consequences. Situations appearing initially to be routine and non-lethal, nonetheless require constant vigilance. Accordingly, the work can be extremely stressful for officers. The FLETC has been a leader in addressing the psychological and physiological factors affecting perceptions, reactions, and performance of law enforcement personnel during realistic and highly stressful training scenarios. In addition to providing students with valuable feedback about their capabilities, insights drawn from this research may be applied to training at the FLETC, and might also be made available to the broader law enforcement community through reports and publications. Clearly, this project will identify training innovations to increase the survivability of the law enforcement officer. The Training Research Branch, Training Innovation Division has developed a sophisticated eight-factor performance analytic matrix, and most recently has been evaluating the efficacy of feedback that is student-centered vs. instructor-centered. The exceptional capabilities and professional experience of the FLETC staff and their ability to work with an interdisciplinary group of scientists from outside of the law enforcement community have made this project a unique and highly successful research effort. I can imagine no other organization capable of doing such research with equal realism, scientific rigor and relevance to the law enforcement professional.

James L. Meyerhoff, M.D.
Adjunct Professor,
Depts. of Psychiatry and Physiology,
Georgetown University School of Medicine
3800 Reservoir Rd., NW
Washington, DC 20007

Table of Contents

SECTION I

Following the STAR to Improve Performance

1

Following the Star to Improve Performance

Organization of the Paper

Section 1 discusses the importance of exploring new methodologies that improve training for law enforcement officers. There is a constant flow of new research that deals with how people learn. When this updated knowledge is combined with new technologies—such as enhanced audio-visual information capabilities—learning opportunities and retention are enhanced. This section provides an overview of the research study; the development of STAR, a new, risk-based scoring system; and a review of how the brain processes information prior to responding to an unknown situation, similar to those faced by law enforcement officers.

Section 2 describes the design of four research scenarios and the eight STAR factors used to measure proficiency in each area. Performance levels for each area are summarized using a risk-based scale; the four scenarios are contrasted by comparing lethal versus non-lethal performance.

Section 3 describes the broad impact emotional stress has on scenario training and how trainers can use this information to design and measure stress levels in their scenarios as well as prepare students for future encounters through stress exposure training.

Section 4 describes the important role feedback has on improving future performance and the numerous factors that should be part of the feedback session. These factors were evaluated in the research scenarios to determine their impact on student performance.

Introduction

"Following a two year decline, law enforcement fatalities in 2010 spiked to 162. This was an increase of nearly 40 percent compared to the previous year when 117 officers were killed in the line of duty" (NLEOMF, 2011). Law enforcement officers/agents routinely encounter situations that require them to make decisions with limited information under rapidly changing conditions. Many of these situations expose officers to inordinate risks, and under certain circumstances, require the use of lethal or non-lethal weapons for defensive or preemptive purposes. FBI research (Federal Bureau of Investigation, 1997) indicates that many assaults on law enforcement personnel were the result of the officer missing or misinterpreting pre-assault indicators. Interviews with offenders convicted of assaulting officers revealed that the victim officers did not present a strong command presence and that the officers did not perceive their assailants as a threat (Federal Bureau of Investigation, 2006). As a training institution, it is our responsibility to provide students with proven instruction and techniques that will enable them to serve their agencies effectively. This paper presents the results of a scenario-based research study that evaluated the application of recently learned law enforcement tactics in novel situations.

Four different scenarios were created to challenge student thinking and actions in order to monitor training effectiveness. This paper includes literature related to the research, newly created or existing assessment tools used to measure student responses, and suggested actions for improvement of future training. Although the term "performance" is used throughout this report, it is the decision making process of the students that dictates what actions will take place. Whether in training or the real world, mental preparation and situation awareness are essential qualities all officers must possess in order to respond effectively.

Using Research to Refine Performance

The Federal Law Enforcement Training Center's (FLETC's) Training Research Branch (TRB) has undertaken several initiatives to incorporate research-based tactics and instruction to improve law enforcement training. The term research-based indicates that a methodology or technology has been measured and validated in its intended environment and has proven itself to be superior through a comparative research study. Once Subject Matter Experts (SMEs) have developed and delivered law enforcement training, it is instructionally sound to evaluate its effectiveness to ensure the training has met the desired expectations and goals. As a law enforcement training center, this means using realistic situations in a real world (realistic scenario) environment. There are multiple elements that contribute to the realism or fidelity of a scenario. These elements and their significance are discussed in detail in Section 3.

Initial Research

In 2000, the FLETC initiated the Survival Scores Research Project (SSRP) whose primary goal was to determine if a scoring system could be developed that would reflect a student's capacity to engage in and survive a lethal encounter. Although students receive a firearms score for their marksmanship in the static Practical Pistol Course, many trainers are of the opinion that some type of "survival score" would better reflect a student's ability to win a force on force confrontation (FLETC, 2004). The SSRP provided novel insight regarding the likelihood of winning a lethal encounter, and provided new strategies for evaluating training and delivering feedback to students about their performance. One objective of the SSRP was to create an evaluation tool that would determine how well students perform their law enforcement skills within the framework of a reality-based training scenario. Another objective of the original study was to confirm that the evaluation instrument could provide the performance assessment in real time. This paper will present the results of a second phase of the SSRP, focus on a new scenario assessment and scoring process, explore the impact of feedback on performance, and explain how mental models are used to guide future performance. During Phase II, the SSRP research team developed a new assessment model—Scenario Training Assessment and Review (STAR). The STAR focuses on the essential elements required to evaluate a student's ability to make decisions under threat conditions and implement those decisions to control the situation.

Building on Initial Research

The FLETC originally embarked on the SSRP in 2000 to test 97 performance elements taught in its basic training programs. Each of the 97 elements was cross-referenced to an instructional objective. A continuous scenario was developed to enable students to demonstrate each of the performance elements. In addition, the scenario was designed to escalate in stress as the student moved from one event to another. Scenario stress levels were validated using a variety of indicators including heart rate, blood pressure, cortisol, and psychological assessments. While the study was highly beneficial to the FLETC in examining law enforcement responses under high stress, student scores were lower than anticipated in several areas.

Creating a New Assessment Model

In 2006, a new research team consisting of law enforcement trainers and subject matter experts from the various training divisions closely examined the 97 performance elements used in the first phase of the SSRP. While examining the performance elements, the subject matter experts realized that most of the scale used to rate the elements were not unique to one training area but were a combination of several training disciplines (e.g., behavioral science, tactics, counterterrorism, vehicle operations, firearms, intermediate weapons). Due to the universal nature of the performance areas, the evaluation scale could be applied to any of the training disciplines. Additionally, the team conducted an extensive review of literature from law enforcement publications, Office of Personnel Management (OPM) competency statements, lessons learned from assaults on officers, reality-based training, and research on decision making under stress. Using information obtained from these varied sources, combined with the universal nature of the 97 performance elements, the subject matter experts grouped the 97 elements into eight areas or

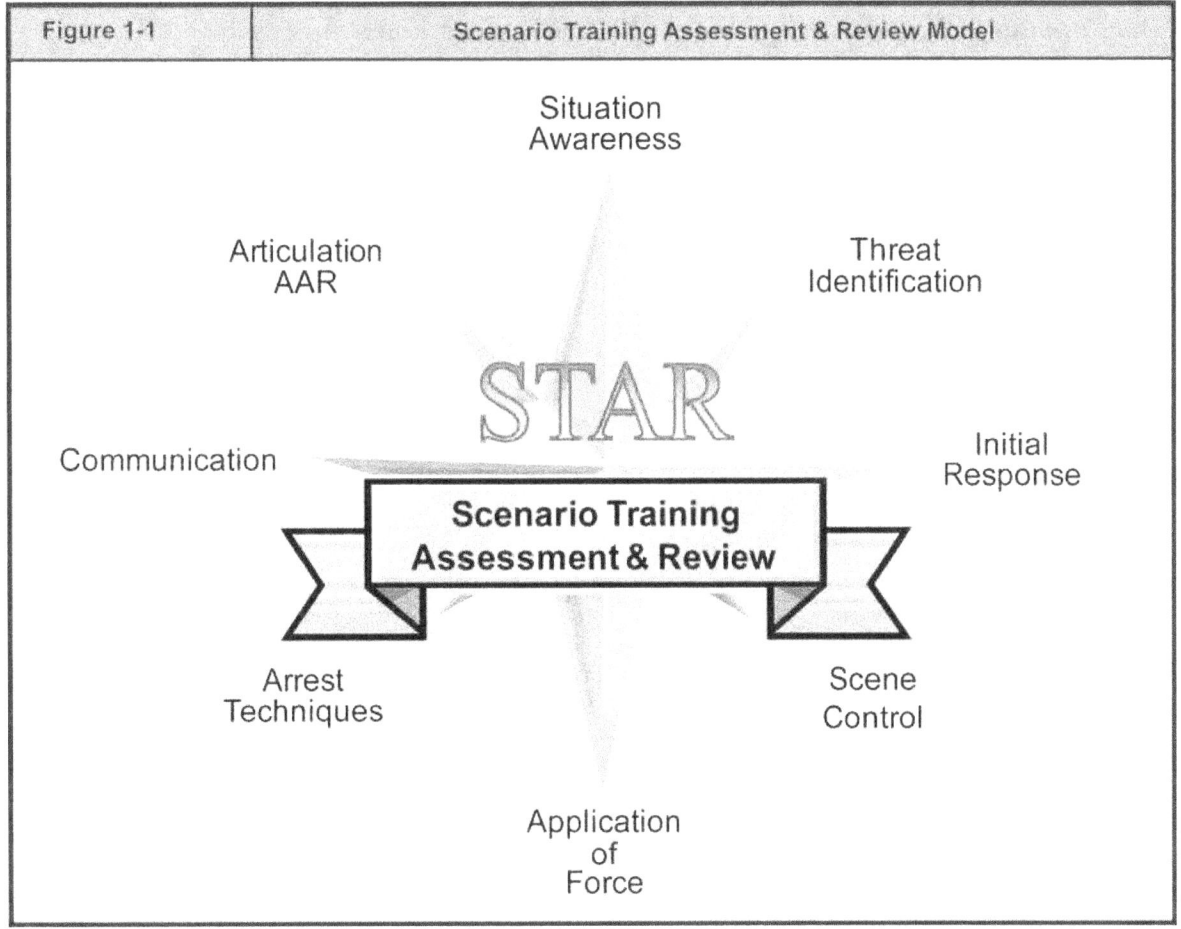

| Figure 1-1 | Scenario Training Assessment & Review Model |

Situation Awareness

Articulation AAR

Threat Identification

STAR

Communication

Initial Response

Scenario Training Assessment & Review

Arrest Techniques

Scene Control

Application of Force

factors to be used for the STAR. The eight STAR factors (Figure 1-1) represent "survival factors" associated with reality-based training scenarios; and each student performance element falls into one of these eight factors. The eight STAR factors and their definitions are:

1. **Situation Awareness**. Being aware of what is happening around you in order to understand how information, events, and your own actions will impact your goals and objectives, both now and in the near future.

2. **Threat Identification**. Accounting for threats and non-threats, properly prioritized, effectively communicated, and appropriate response is efficiently planned.

3. **Initial Response.** A strategy to counter any threat or emergency situation and includes the position of advantage, tactics, or other corrective actions.

4. **Scene Control (**following the *Initial Response*). The ability to maintain control of the situation including evidence, crime scene, threats, victims, and witnesses.

5. **Application of Force.** Application of appropriate/timely force options and articulation consistent with the Constitutional standard.

6. **Arrest Techniques.** Initiation of correct procedures during an arrest including position of disadvantage, handcuffing, and search.

7. **Communication.** Information exchange between entities through correct/timely verbal commands, non-verbal behaviors, and written accounts.

8. **Articulation/After Action Review** (AAR). Providing factual/accurate information during a scenario debriefing session.

For continuity of mental preparation, students should become familiar with the eight performance factors and begin to think of their responses within this framework. Thus, entering a building to clear it (taught by Enforcement Operations Division), the student should mentally rehearse and execute *"situation awareness"* (defined on p. 1-12). Additionally, when responding to domestic disputes (taught by Behavioral Sciences Division) officers should utilize situation awareness such as engaging the victim and others from a safe vantage point. The task of removing a suspect from a vehicle with multiple occupants (taught by the Driver and Marine Division) requires situation awareness and other factors as well. The first two factors of the STAR emphasize mental preparation and should remind officers to "analyze" and "develop" a strategy prior to making contact. The universal nature of the eight factors should enable students to readily adapt and apply them to most real world situations.

The evaluation process for determining successful scenario performance was another area identified by the research team as needing modification. In the initial research study it was common for students to receive failing scores on several performance items yet still pass the scenario. For example, though many students failed to use the classroom-demonstrated process for clearing their weapon, they successfully cleared the weapon and continued to engage the suspect. Evaluators grappled with the issue of whether students should fail the exercise (for not successfully performing a trained skill) or merely have a point deducted since the overall goal was achieved. When evaluating the performance of a skill, the evaluator typically compares the student performance to the performance used in the class demonstration. It was obvious to the research team that, although the performance fell short of the desired "gold standard" of execution, the discrepancy did not warrant a failing grade.

Risk Based Scoring

A new "survival index" was created to more accurately capture the spectrum of student performance ranging from unacceptable to desirable. The new scoring index would also provide a more accurate and objective basis for feedback and mentoring of students and reflect the students' likelihood of winning a threat encounter. The survival index was based upon the comparison of risks associated with the performance, and how the students' actions reduced the likelihood and severity of harm. Establishing an objective scale for risk assessment is a formidable task due to the fact that risk levels are interpreted differently by each individual. A general definition of risk for this study is, "Risk is uncertainty about and severity of the consequences (or outcomes) of an activity with respect to something that humans value" (Aven, 2006). Clearly defined actions and responses were used as indicators of decision making, perception of the level of threat, individual vulnerabilities, potential consequences, and the resulting degree of anxiety.

In developing a risk assessment scale, a team of SMEs thoroughly reviewed each scenario and identified those objects, situations, individuals, etc., that could cause harm, particularly to the officer/agent. After identifying each risk, the team determined how likely and severe the risk was, and then weighted the measures appropriately. In this manner, a more precise system of scoring was created that also provided more complete and detailed feedback to the student, and rendered a more realistic "survival score". The resulting risk-based scale can now award points for less than perfect performance as well as differentiate between the various levels of risk-based performance. The assessment scale for scoring student performance used a "0 to 4" Likert scale. Table 1-1 identifies each rating and provides a brief description of applicable student actions.

Table 1-1	Scenario Performance Assessment Scale
Rating	**Description**
0. Not Applicable	does not apply or is not observable
1. Not Acceptable	actions are not consistent with legal standard, creates serious risk, or did not perform
2. Least Desirable	actions generally acceptable but create identifiable risks
3. Acceptable	actions are consistent with training but not most effective method or tactic
4. Desirable	actions demonstrate sound and effective tactics

An example of this type of rating would be to award students a "4" (Desirable) if they successfully and timely performed a "Tap, Rack" during a weapon malfunction requiring a primary immediate action procedure; "3" (Acceptable) if they cleared the malfunction in a timely manner but failed to "Tap" before racking the slide; "2" (Least Desirable) if they failed to recognize the weapon malfunction in a timely manner or took an extended amount of time to clear the malfunction; or"1" (Not Acceptable) if they required multiple attempts or failed to clear the weapon.

The elements of the scenario performance checklist generate the training factors associated with the STAR. The elements identified with each STAR factor are typically unique to the scenario. For example, elements of "Situation Awareness" should reflect the location and other specific cues presented during the scenario. This supports specific scenario behaviors while maintaining the contextual reference to a STAR factor.

Using the eight factors of reality-based scenario performance, the STAR provided an effective tool for evaluation and feedback Articulation/After Action Review (AAR) for law enforcement students participating in four novel scenarios. The term "novel" is used to describe a scenario whose specific design (lethal or non-lethal; number of role players and their degree of compliance) are unknown to the student. Perfect performance and a perfect score are not requirements for a successful outcome. However, it is essential that students demonstrate critical knowledge and skills associated with scenario performance objectives. The STAR is an effective way to mentally plan prior to responding to a call, as well as measure competencies in a law enforcement training scenario. Mental planning and decision making are critical skills needed by all law enforcement officers in order to conduct safe and effective arrests and avoid taking unnecessary risks. A common challenge for every training institution is to provide students with sound decision making skills during basic training that will prepare them for their future careers.

Building Mental Models

One of the most common frameworks used to describe the various levels of mental processing was developed by educators in the 1950s to rank mental tasks from simple to complex (Bloom, 1956). The classification of mental processing into various levels of complexity enables instructors to design learning experiences for a specific level of thinking such as simple recall (what does the term "bolo" mean) versus higher level thinking such as

Table 1-2		Cognitive Domain Classification
	Level	Description
6 (complex)	Evaluation	Appraise or critique on the basis of a specific standard or criteria.
5	Synthesis	Integrate information into an original plan or product specific to that situation.
4	Analysis	Distinguish or classify the basic evidence or assumptions of a statement or question.
3	Knowledge	Recalls or recognizes information, ideas, principles in the general way they were learned.
2	Comprehension	Interprets or comprehends information based upon prior learning.
1 (simple)	Application	Uses and transfers information and principles to complete a task with little or no assistance.

analysis (after reading a case file, describe whether the officer's search was reasonable and state reasons why). The second example would require the recall of specific legal guidelines and the ability to determine if all legal requirements were met. The classification system for mental processing was termed the "Cognitive Domain" and placed mental processing on a scale from simple to complex as shown in Table 1-2. Educators also identified two other domains (not presented in this paper), the affective domain and the psychomotor domain, as additional areas whose classification would help instructors develop learning activities. The affective domain focuses on how the body responds emotionally through values and attitudes; the psychomotor domain focuses on how the body responds physically through motor skills and performance. One of the goals for classifying mental skills into various levels was to ensure that students would receive training on many levels of mental processing rather than at the simplest levels. When students are competent in the basics, they are then ready to apply them to new and more challenging situations.

Dr. Ruth Clark (2008) in her book *Building Expertise* uses a terminology that is unlike that used in the cognitive domain, to compare simple mental tasks (known as near transfer) to complex tasks (far transfer), as shown in Table 1-3. When new information and skills are

Table 1-3		Levels of Transfer
	Level	Description
3 (complex)	Far - Transfer	Creation of new solutions not addressed in training; ability to solve ill-defined tasks not presented in training, such as controlling suspects in novel situations.
2	Moderate - Transfer	Transfer of skills to new situations not encountered in training, able to handcuff highly resistive suspect in confined space.
1 (simple)	Near - Transfer	Students successfully pass handcuffing skills test, and proficiently perform handcuffing 3 months later on the job.
0	Zero - Transfer	Students successfully pass handcuffing skills test, but are unable to perform handcuffing 3 months later on the job.

learned, the brain forms mental models for future use. If that information is needed the following day in a manner identical to the way it was learned, that is called a "near transfer" of the information. Near-transfer tasks are typically procedures that require no interpretation or analysis - just simple recall. Moderate transfer allows the student to go beyond the basic application of knowledge by applying information to a new setting or a variation of a previous problem. Far-transfer recall requires the learner to solve non-routine problems through innovative thinking. Effective training programs should be designed to guide students through the process of reinforcing skills so that they can be stored in long-term memory for future use. The next step is to allow learners to build on existing knowledge by using it in new situations. This facilitates the transfer of knowledge to novel situations and enhances flexible thinking for future situations that have not been previously experienced. This process will eventually lead to creative thinking or far-transfer which enables individuals to solve complex problems despite never having observed them previously. The terms near-transfer and far-transfer take the learning process a step beyond merely classifying mental capabilities; it identifies how mental processing is enhanced and viable solutions become real-time decisions on the job. This is a critical component for all law enforcement training programs.

In order to develop near-transfer and far-transfer skills, law enforcement training should be designed to provide students with realistic problems and solutions. Although the number of situations and suspects encountered by law enforcement officers is virtually limitless, training can provide the officer with essential memories and decision making skills to develop moderate-transfer and far-transfer skills for these novel situations.

The Impact of Mental Models on Decision Making

When circumstances present a threatening situation that is also new to the individual, the average individual does not possess sufficient pre-programmed responses to react effectively to the threatening situation. Colonel John Boyd described the steps that all human beings go through before making a decision on a course of action—whether the situation is a dynamic high-risk encounter or a routine activity (Plehn, 2000). These sequential steps are Observe, Orient, Decide, and Act and are frequently referred to as "Boyd's Loop" or the "OODA Loop". The first step of observation involves being aware of what is happening around you in order to understand how information, events, and your own actions will impact your goals and objectives. This is often referred to as "situation awareness," which is essentially being aware of what is happening around you. Orientation is the second and critical step where analysis and synthesis of the observations occur. It is here that the various facts are sorted out and a mental picture of the situation is formed. The true test of the OODA loop occurs during a high-risk situation when the final two steps (decide and act) must be performed quickly under stress with the risk of severe consequences. The concept of Boyd's Loop (Schechtman, 1996) provides a plausible answer as to why students, during a challenging scenario, often appear to be "stuck" (both physically and mentally) for a lengthy period of time and take no further action. When officers/agents lack experiential memories from either real-life or training, they routinely get stuck between the "observe" and "orient" steps. They get stuck because they have not developed mental models necessary to rapidly interpret the situation (moderate transfer) and then decide on an appropriate course of action. The goal of training, and more specifically law enforcement or military training, is to repeatedly expose individuals to unique situations in order for them to develop experiential learning (moderate or far transfer) which will create neural shortcuts and facilitate decisive action. It is through the repeated exposure to novel events (sometimes termed experiential training) that individuals improve their ability to move through the decision phase, and are able to reduce the time needed to select an appropriate action.

Klein's work (2004) has confirmed Boyd's premise and characterizes indecision or being "stuck" as simply an insufficient number of repeated experiences. It is the repeated exposure to similar situations that create the mental linking of memories which can then be recalled in the future when encountering a situation with similar elements. The repeated exposure to similar situations facilitates the rapid assessment of the situation even when information is limited. Conversely, when officers face a unique situation and the number of mental associations stored in memory are limited, then little or no transfer will take place leading to a delayed or inappropriate decision.

Augmenting the Mental Model

Situation awareness is defined as being aware of what is happening around you in order to understand how information, events, and your own actions will impact your goals and objectives—both now and in the near future (Endsley, Bolte, and Jones, 2003) (Endsley and Robertson, 2000). Situation awareness is a technique commonly taught in high-risk professions (military, public safety, aviation) that provides a framework for evaluating an environment for factors that may contribute to the level of threat or danger. These factors or cues are acquired through sight, sound, smell, touch, or taste. Some cues, like building alarms, are obvious while others, like facial expressions, are more subtle and may only register subconsciously. Situation awareness enables officers/agents to function in a timely and effective manner. When individuals become more skilled using situation awareness, they are able to more rapidly assess the level of a threat and decide whether to proceed or retreat. Research studies have also pointed out a positive relationship between situational awareness levels and scenario performance levels (Cannon-Bowers, Salas, and Converse, 2001).

A second technique that enhances decision making transfer is contextual reference. Contextual references are the interrelated factors or conditions that are associated with a situation; it is the setting. Contextual elements can make a scenario more realistic by adding sounds, smells, clothing, etc., that tend to increase the believability and realism of the scene. Contextual references are also part of situation awareness and are able to tell officers what is out of place or abnormal in a particular setting, and whether a re-evaluation of the situation is prudent. One of the most critical skills that law enforcement officers must develop is the ability to interpret a situation and assess the degree of risk.

Transferring Skills to Real Life

What has been generally observed in TRB research is that students tend to use a concept only in the specific setting in which it was learned, which indicates only near-transfer. This is to say, if situation awareness is only taught in enforcement operations, it is rarely observed (transferred/applied) in other contexts, such as arrest techniques or vehicle stops. This narrow application of a universal concept must change. The following examples shows how cognitive skills such as situation awareness and contextual references must be taught in basic training and reinforced on the job in order for them to be second nature on the job.

When training law enforcement students to conduct a high-risk vehicle stop and direct a known felon out of the driver's seat of a vehicle, a very specific sequence of steps is required. These steps require the student to command the driver to perform specific actions that facilitate the safe removal of the driver from the vehicle, as well as provide officer safety to the student. However, if the arrest is performed alongside a busy interstate, other factors must be incorporated into the plan for making contact with the felon. Obviously, understanding the totality of the situation (situation awareness) is just as important as the sequence of steps. Another example is an officer responding to a domestic violence complaint. If the officer arrives during a spousal dispute and finds a battered female and an aggressive male, the officer typically focuses on the perceived threat of the male attacker. When this occurs, research indicates that the officer often ignores the threat the female victim may pose. This particular scenario has proven fatal to officers in the past who failed to properly assess the context and threat level posed by both individuals. Law enforcement training must include strategies for creating mental models that will guide officers in the evaluation of risk in a situation and the development of safe and effective tactics in the performance of their duties.

Summary

A critical component of officer safety and survival is the ability to make effective decisions under stress. This capacity is most critical in those situations that rapidly escalate to the point at which an immediate and appropriate response is necessary for survival. Cognitive processing and preparation are critical skills that must also be a part of law enforcement training. The STAR provides a reminder that mental preparation is critical to success and survivability. The STAR is also an effective tool for evaluating students' selection of appropriate responses and their execution during realistic, stressful, and dynamic encounters.

The STAR offers several benefits to the trainer. The first is the development of a standardized evaluation and feedback tool that is based upon eight factors, making it much more practical than its predecessor. The STAR was tested in four different scenarios and provided an easy method for systematic feedback that covered the eight performance factors. The consistent use of the STAR factors also facilitated training continuity when discussed in feedback/AAR sessions.

The second benefit of using the STAR process is that it was able to provide more consistent scoring by the evaluators due to the objective, risk-based scale. The risk-based scale provides a more effective indication of students' competency by utilizing an expanded scale as opposed to merely a pass/fail system. Possibly just as important, the scale provides the instructor with more detailed information for the feedback/AAR session and the determination of the student's strengths and areas of improvement. The findings in this study suggest that the adoption of the STAR will provide more complete training and will produce better-prepared officers and agents. The findings also suggest that the adoption of the STAR will ensure more effective and consistent assessment of student performance during scenario based training. Effective implementation of the STAR will require training in these techniques and would extend to instructor training programs that utilize scenario-based training.

Intentionally left blank

SECTION II

Student Performance During Stressful Scenarios

2

Student Performance During Stressful Scenarios

Caveat

Before presenting a description of the four research scenarios, it is imperative to understand that one of the primary goals of this study was to evaluate the impact of various environmental and circumstantial stressors on performance. These stressors impact cognitive processing through the acquisition of danger signals, identifying suspects and potential actions while scanning for visual and auditory cues. These factors have been placed in scenarios at specific points to evaluate cognitive processing and responses, as opposed to simply developing scenarios to evaluate competency of law enforcement skills. All students in this study have previously demonstrated competency in all basic law enforcement knowledge and skills. It is hoped that this work will contribute to a more rapid detection and response to subtle cues and factors that are typically acquired after years of experience on the job. A long-term goal for this research endeavor is to accelerate the learning process for law enforcement trainees and increase their "survivability." The research team of SMEs believes that this work will assist the FLETC in developing training programs that benefit both law enforcement trainees and officers in the field; and, ultimately save lives.

Transfer of Training to the Real World

Law enforcement agencies, including the FBI and the National Institute of Justice, have recorded and analyzed crime report data over time to better understand the causes of felonious assaults on law enforcement officers. These data have been correlated to identify meaningful trends that can be used to guide the development of law enforcement training. When analyzing violent encounters, the FBI typically reviews and records the data as seen through three distinct vantage points: the offender, the officer, and the circumstances. In the 2006 report, a new topic—officer perception—was added that focused on using officer perceptions to increase officer safety. As mentioned in Section I of this report, scenario training should be designed to expose officers to novel situations (circumstances) that include an offender, and enhance the decision making process in a rapidly evolving environment. Dr. Darrell Ross, a university researcher who has written in the area of lethal encounters, has expanded upon the three elements found in the NIJ Report to include a fourth element, the *environment* (Ross, 2008).

As a Professor and Department Head of Criminal Justice at Valdosta State University, Dr. Ross has served as an expert witness involving lethal force incidents for over ten years. In his research article on lethal force encounters, Ross reviewed the cases of 125 officers who survived lethal-force confrontations. He found one critical factor missing from the three key factors listed in the NIJ Report: environment. The more realistic the training preparation (using realistic scenarios and environments that provide patterns and trends with contextual factors), the more effective is the response to lethal force encounters. In addition to providing realistic scenarios that facilitate decision making skills, Dr. Ross listed additional characteristics as keys to winning violent confrontations: mental preparation, awareness of danger signals, timely reaction and transition time, decisive action, multi-task under pressure, and ability to explain circumstances. In order to perform effectively under stress, law enforcement training should strive to provide stressful encounters that replicate challenging, real-life situations and environments. As Dr. Ross concluded in the review of the 125 officers, "Training, practice, and experience leads to less severity of symptoms associated with perceptual distortions." The research team concurs with Dr. Ross' conclusions and made every effort to incorporate the elements of mental preparation, awareness of danger signals, timely reaction and transition time, decisive action, multi-task under pressure, and ability to explain circumstances into the design of the research scenarios and the STAR factors.

Scenario Development and Procedures

Four research scenarios were developed in order to measure student performance in a realistic environment. Virtually all of the characteristics previously mentioned as keys to winning a violent encounter were utilized in the development of each scenario. Law enforcement students who satisfactorily completed all coursework and training at the FLETC volunteered as participants for the study. There were 49 male and 9 female students who ranged in age from 23 to 56 years with a mean age of 29.8. Education and ethnic/racial backgrounds were diverse. In order to compare performance scores to the lethality of the scenario, the 58 students performed two lethal force scenarios (Active Shooter and Armed Robbery) and two non-lethal force scenarios (Trespasser and Attorney). The four scenarios were administered over a consecutive two-day period and are described in detail in Appendix 2.

Prior to Scenario One (Response to Active Shooter), students received a pre-brief from an instructor. Immediately following each scenario, students were seated in an interview room and completed a questionnaire that recorded the self-reported anger and anxiety levels (discussed Section III) they experienced during the scenario. Upon completion of the questionnaire, an instructor provided feedback to students regarding their performance during the scenario.

Prior to the start of Scenario Two (Non-compliant Trespassing Protestor), students received the scenario pre-brief. Following the second scenario, students again completed the anger and anxiety questionnaire, received feedback on their performance, and received a situational awareness (SA) interview conducted by a FLETC instructor. During the SA interview, students were asked to recall details from the shoot scenario in order to determine their ability to articulate facts, the accuracy and detail of their recall, and understand their perception and thought process during the scenario. Based upon the level of detail provided by students, the instructor would then ask more specific questions in order to collect additional details. Instructors typically used follow-up questions such as "How many people were present?" "How many threats were there?" The additional questions about scenario details that were missed provided additional insight as to student perception and thinking process.

On the following day, two new scenarios were used. Scenario Three was a Non-compliant Attorney and Scenario Four was an Armed Robbery in Progress scenario. All four scenarios reflected similar fact patterns and required execution of basic law enforcement skills.

Scenario Scoring

The research team used the eight STAR factors (Figure 2-1) for evaluating scenario performance. The STAR factors provided a consistent scoring process for the research team through the use of the "degree of risk" scale (Table 2-1) developed for scenario performance. Measurement of training skills can be very difficult. Even when actions are clearly observed and reflect the judgment of the officer, obtaining a consistent performance score between evaluators can be difficult to obtain due to differences in an officer's *perception* of the level of threat,

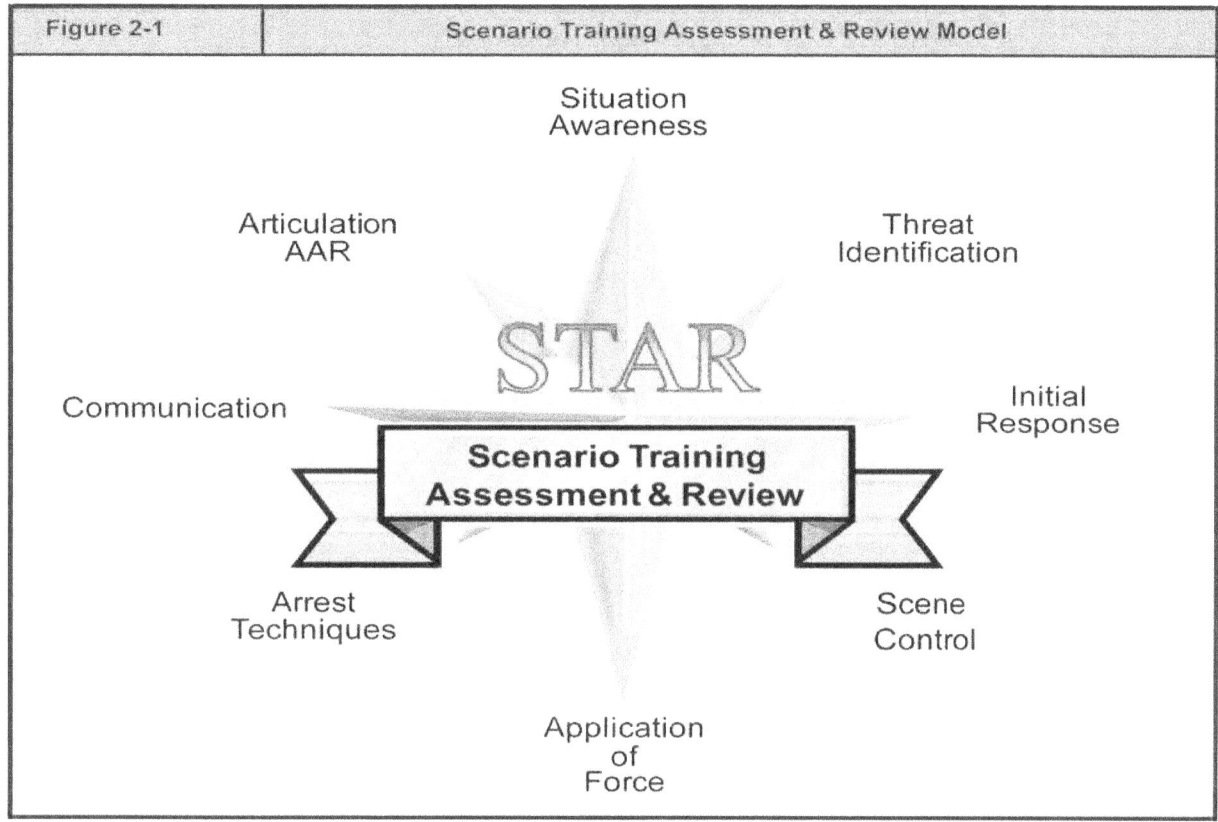

Figure 2-1	Scenario Training Assessment & Review Model

individual vulnerabilities, and potential consequences. The research team used this scale to evaluate each student's ability to win the encounter during each of the stressful scenarios.

Table 2-1	Scenario Performance Assessment Scale
Rating	**Description**
0. Not applicable	does not apply or is not observable.
1. Not acceptable	actions are not consistent with legal standard, creates serious risk, or did not perform.
2. Least desirable	actions generally acceptable but create identifiable risks.
3. Acceptable	actions are consistent with training but not most effective method or tactic, and
4. Desirable	actions demonstrate sound and effective tactics.

Summary Ratings for the Four Scenarios

Figure 2-2 provides an illustration summarizing the average ratings for each scenario. Each of the four scenarios listed at the bottom of the chart has its own box-graph directly above it showing the respective high, average, and low value for each scenario. The color/rating scale shown on the vertical axis provides a numerical and visual indication of the overall performance levels observed for each scenario. Blue (4 rating) indicates the "most desirable" performance level; green (3 rating) indicates performance that is rated "acceptable"; gold (2 rating) reflects performance scored as "least desirable"; and brown (1 rating) represents performance levels that

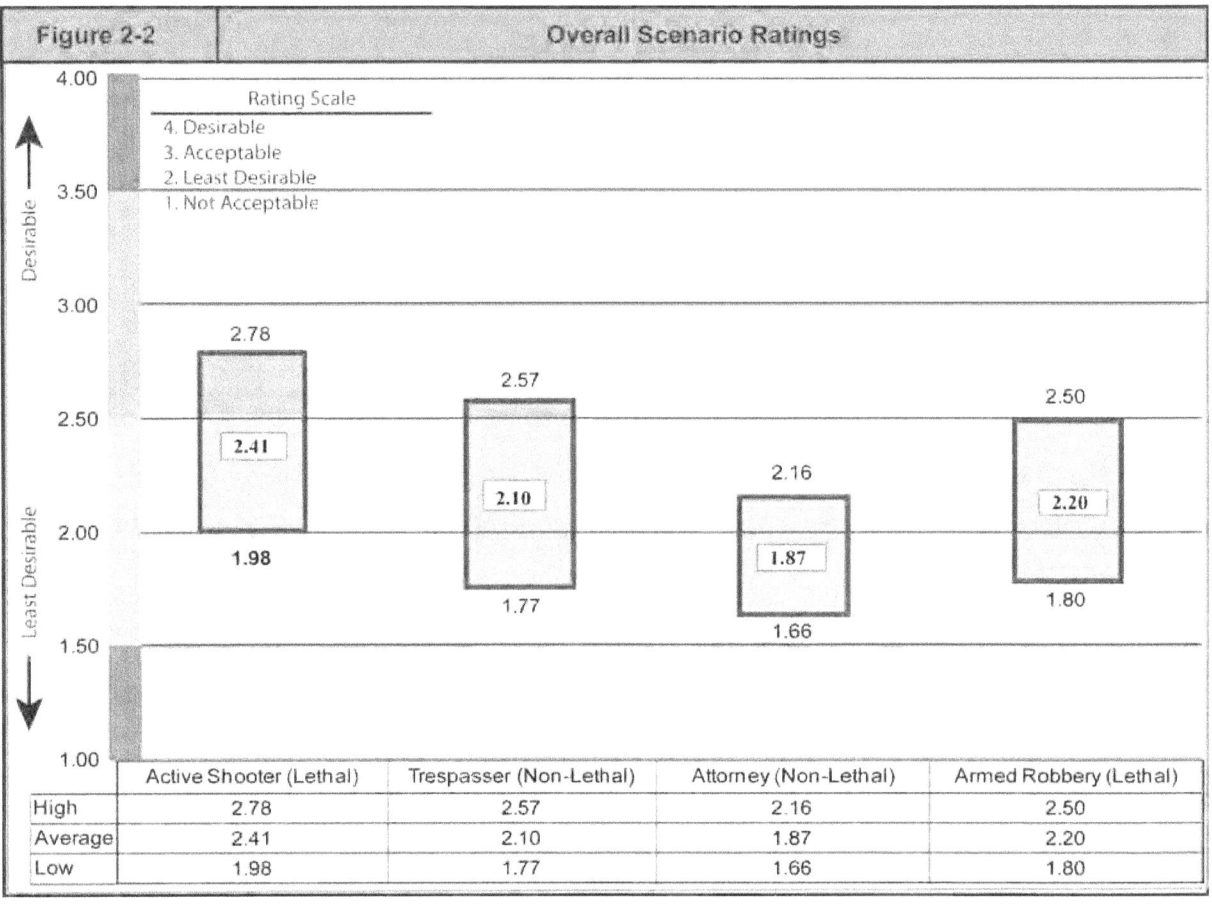

Figure 2-2	Overall Scenario Ratings		
	Active Shooter (Lethal)	Trespasser (Non-Lethal)	Attorney (Non-Lethal)	Armed Robbery (Lethal)
High	2.78	2.57	2.16	2.50
Average	2.41	2.10	1.87	2.20
Low	1.98	1.77	1.66	1.80

were rated "not acceptable". The Active Shooter scenario had the highest average score with an average rating of 2.41, and the Armed Robbery scenario had the second highest score, followed by the two non-lethal scenarios: Trespasser and Attorney. The Active Shooter and Trespasser scenarios contained several elements typically experienced during training. While the Armed Robbery scenario had fact patterns similar to the Active Shooter scenario, it included the additional challenge of a second armed suspect. The Attorney scenario presented the most novel experience and included multiple threats, one of which was a non-compliant authority figure.

Figure 2-3 summarizes the average ratings in each STAR performance factor. Average ratings for Situation Awareness (2.43) and Interview (2.45) were the highest STAR factors. The

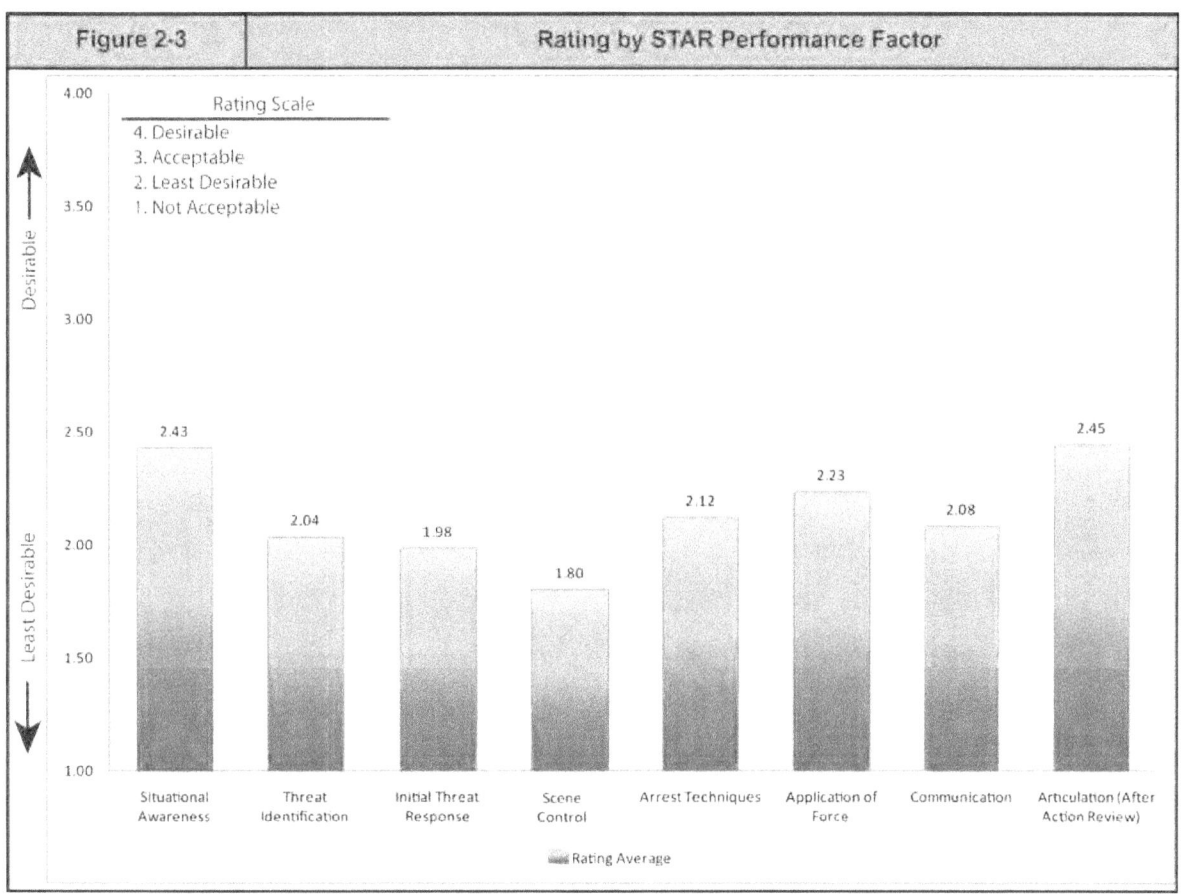

STAR factor Scene Control had the lowest rating average (1.80) and was the lowest rated STAR factor during all four scenarios. Linear regression, used to identify which STAR factors best predict the value of the overall scenario rating, showed that Scene Control ratings account for 86 percent of the variation in overall scenario scores. The three best predictors of the overall scenario score were Control, Situation Awareness, and Initial Threat Response. The combination of these three STAR factors accounts for 95 percent of the overall scenario score variability. Implications of each STAR factor are presented later in this paper.

Figure 2-4 provides a comparison of the combined lethal and combined non-lethal scenario scores. Performance scores for three of the STAR factors were significantly higher during the lethal versus non-lethal scenarios. The three factors were: Initial Threat Response, Application of Force, and Communication. The combined eight STAR ratings during the two

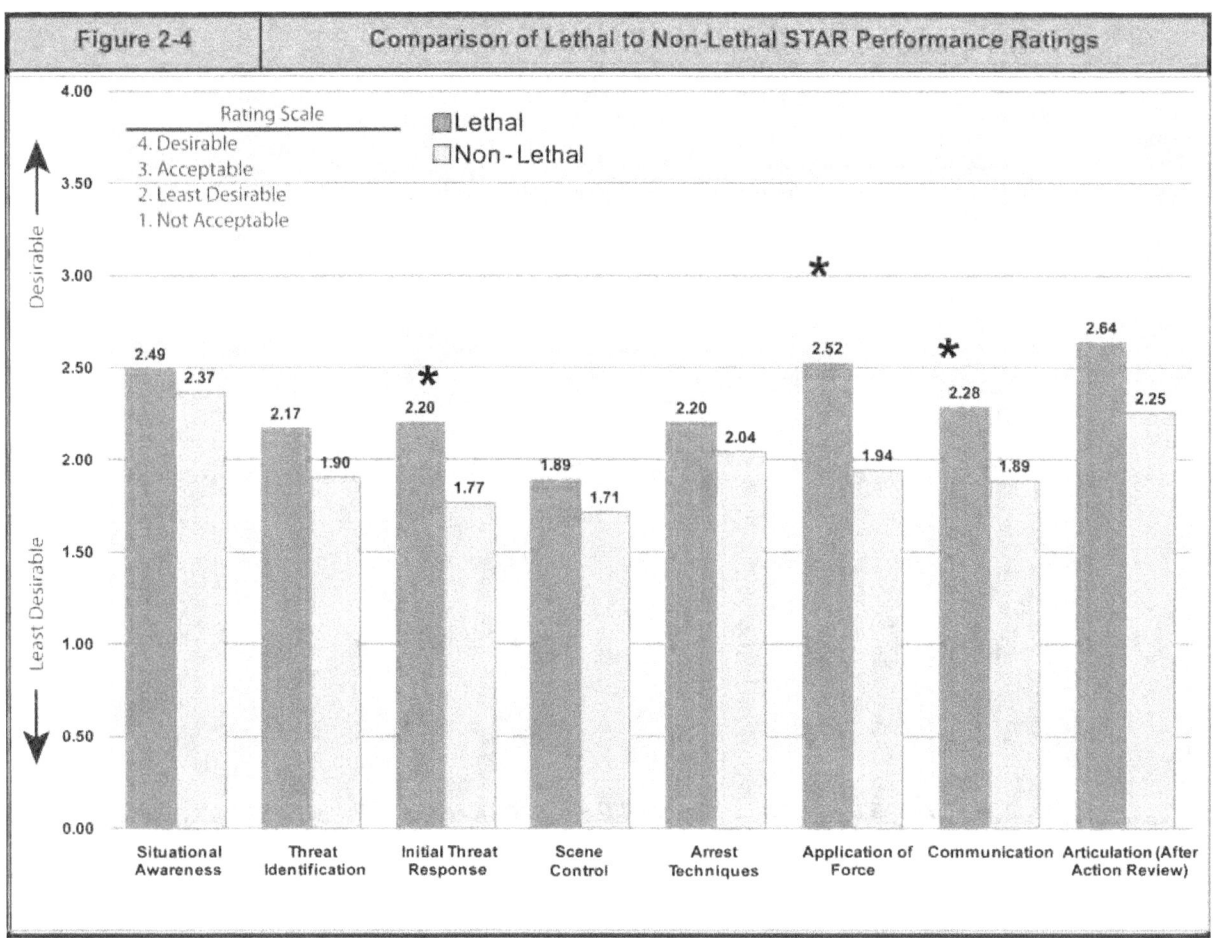

lethal force scenarios (Active Shooter/Armed Robbery = 2.30) were higher than the overall STAR ratings during the two non-lethal force scenarios (Trespasser/Attorney = 1.98). More specifically, lethal scenarios provided better scores on all STAR factors when compared to non-lethal scenarios. Possible explanations for the scoring differences in scoring include: students anticipate lethal force encounters when wearing protective gear, basic training typically culminates with lethal encounters (recent exposure), basic training provides an increased awareness of the most critical encounter – a lethal encounter (heightened awareness and retention), and students receive less exposure to non-lethal situations than lethal situations.

The following pages focus on the eight STAR factors and summarize the performance ratings for the four scenarios. A more detailed analysis for each STAR factor can be found in Appendix 3.

Situation Awareness Observations

Figure 2-5 shows the performance ratings for "Situation Awareness" (student is/is not aware of potential threats) during each scenario. The blue, green, gold, and brown segments reflect the percentage of students who received a rating of "Desirable, Acceptable, Least Desirable, and Not Acceptable" respectively. Students displayed their best situation awareness during the Active Shooter scenario and the lowest performance score was recorded in the Attorney scenario with 41.39 percent of the students having received a "Not Acceptable" rating.

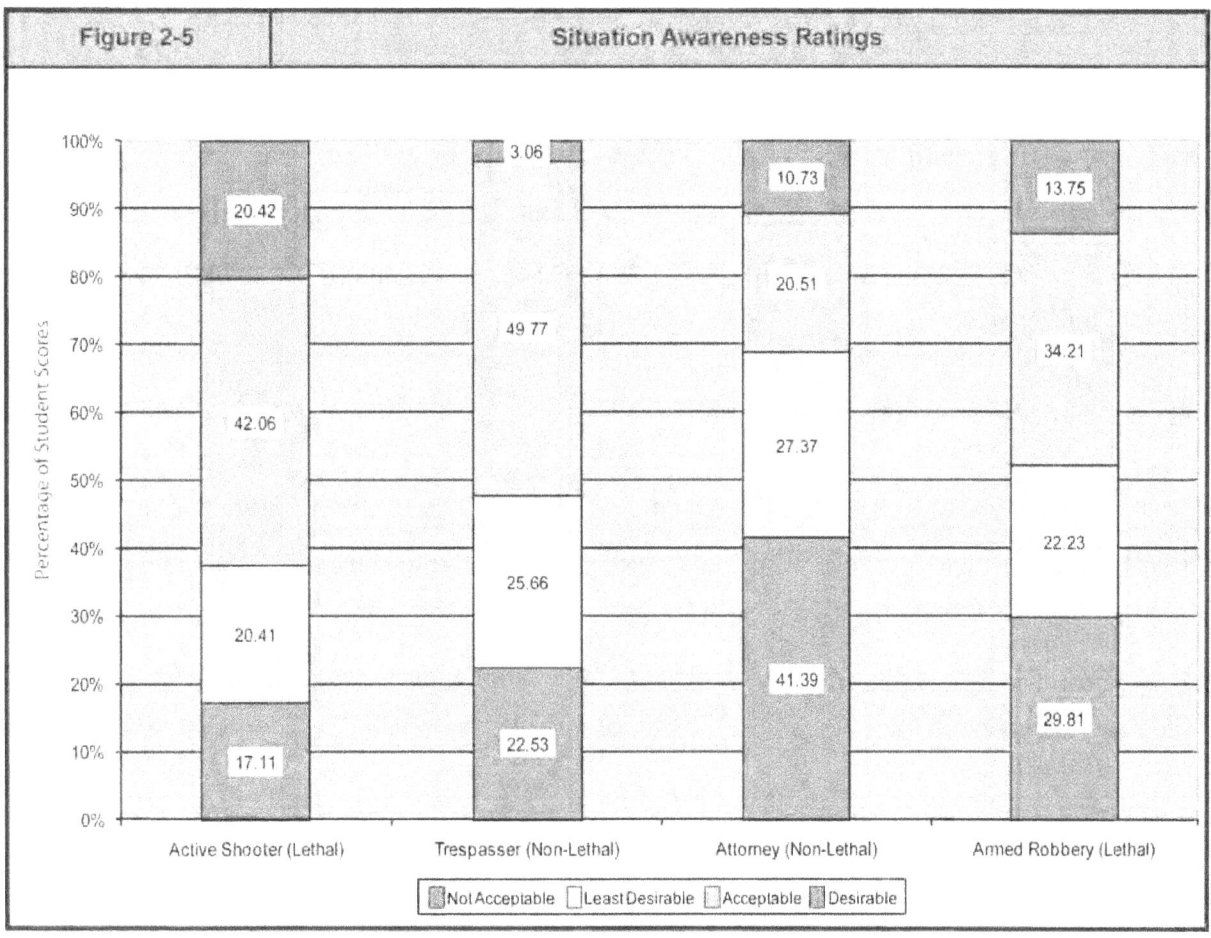

| Figure 2-5 | Situation Awareness Ratings |

As indicated earlier, students performed better in single-threat encounters when compared to scenarios having multiple-threat and/or decisions. When presented with multiple threats or risks, students tended to stop scanning and fix their focus on the initial threat. Students generally had difficulty recognizing and responding to various cues during the initial part of each scenario which would suggest being stuck between the "observe" and "orient" steps of Boyd's Loop.

Situation Awareness Training Implications

Situation awareness (discussed in Section I) requires perceiving critical factors in the environment and understanding what those factors mean. An officer/agent needs to detect threats, interpret victim and witness positions and actions, and identify environmental features and obstacles. Poor situation awareness commonly leads to flawed decision making, errors, and vulnerability. Students have a tendency to focus on the initial threat and fail to scan and assess the area for additional threats and changes in the environment. Officers can get "tunnel vision" focusing on a primary cue and forgetting to scan for additional cues.

The research team suggests that use-of-force training scenarios should incorporate situations utilizing multiple role-players who represent threats, witnesses, and victims. This type of "crowded" scenario would train students to conduct a thorough scan of the environment and determine if there are multiple threats. This could then lead to proper positioning for the potential threat areas.

Threat Identification Observations

Figure 2-6 shows the percentage of student "Threat Identification" (student does/does not properly identify threats) ratings during each scenario. The figure shows that student threat identification was best performed in the Active Shooter scenario and the poorest performance in the Attorney scenario. Many of the students did not respond appropriately to pre-assault indicators and others did not perceive a threat presented by "other persons" in the area.

Threat Identification Training Implications

In Threat Identification, students demonstrated difficulty with identifying secondary threats and prioritizing multiple threats. This difficulty was particularly noticeable during the Attorney and Armed Robbery scenarios. One of the underlying objectives incorporated into the

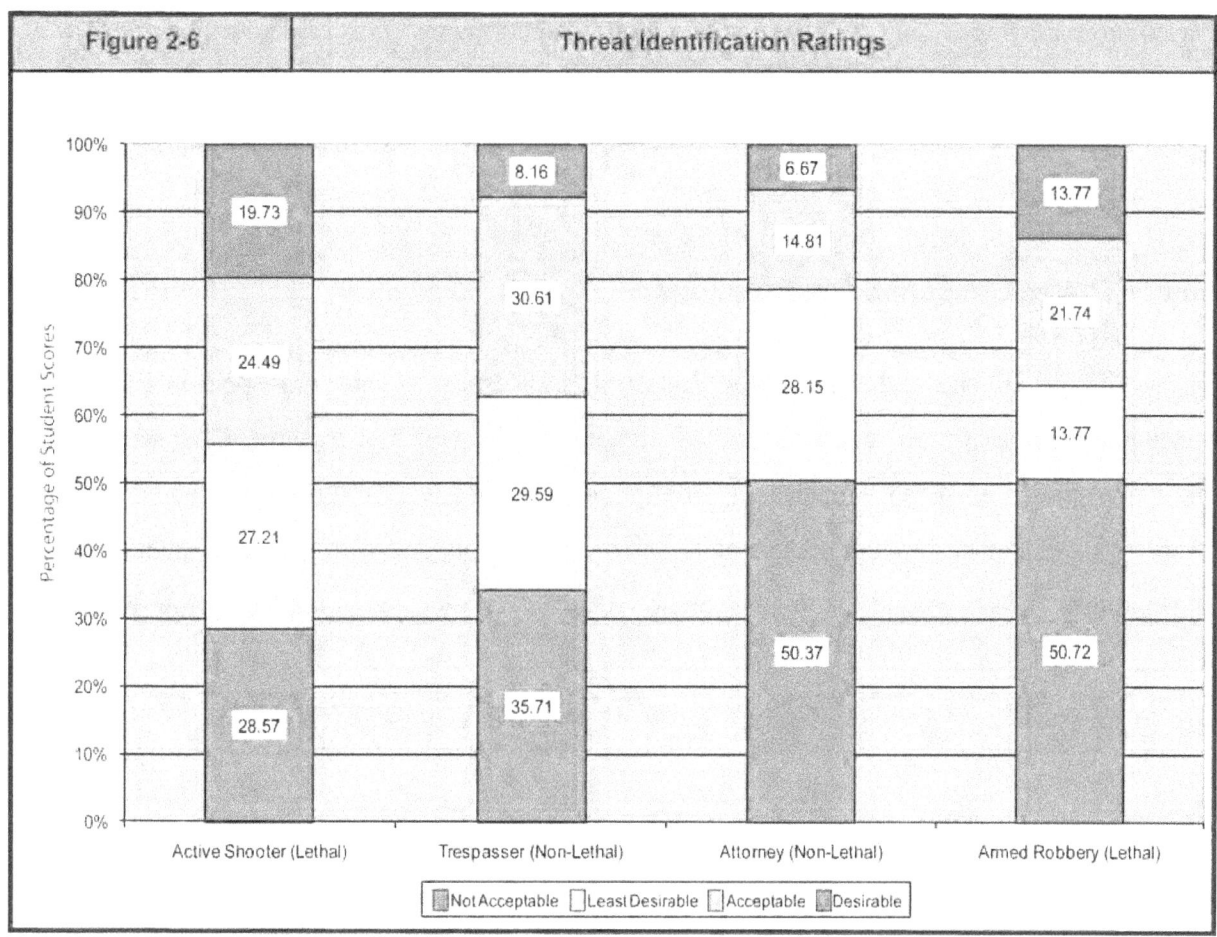

design of each scenario was for students to exert their will (officer/authority presence) over the role-players—especially those who represent threats. To accomplish this, students must develop and execute a plan that engages the threats more quickly than the threats can engage them. One of the most common ways to do this is to use visual and auditory cues to classify the situation as a threat or non-threat and then proceed. The difficulties observed in the Attorney and Armed Robbery scenarios were likely the result of insufficient exposure to situations that require scanning. When an officer/agent is uncertain as to the number, type, and location of threats, it is likely there will either be no action (stuck in Boyd's Loop) or the action will be unplanned. Either option is unacceptable.

The research team recommends creating the right experiences and memories through multiple, reality-based training scenarios. These experiences can help officers/agents develop mechanisms (like Boyd's Loop) to overcome these incapacitating liabilities. The scenarios should include multiple suspects and threats to develop mental models of threat assessment based upon incomplete information and elements of uncertainty. This type of training will develop the skill of rapid threat assessment and establish mental models for future use. This type of training is not limited to new officers as veteran officers will lose this ability unless routinely used or practiced.

Initial Threat Response Observations

Figure 2-7 shows the ratings for "Initial Threat Response" (proper response to threats) during each scenario. The chart reveals that threat response was higher in the lethal scenarios compared to the non-lethal scenarios. Although performance was better in the lethal scenarios, there was a tendency for students to stand in an open doorway and wait for the suspect to shoot at them first. It was not until students watched the video of their performance during the

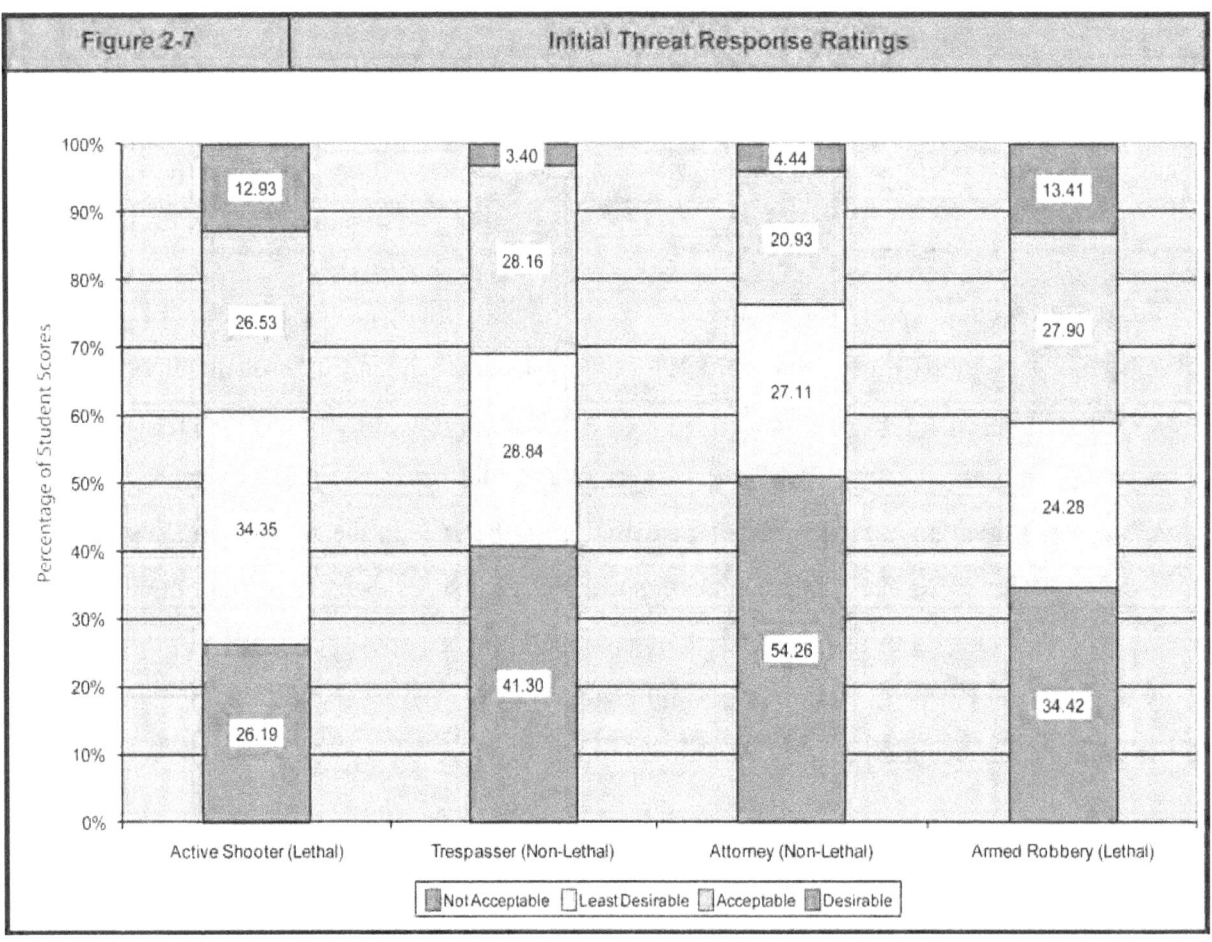

feedback session that they realized how exposed they were in the doorway to the suspect. This distortion of perception is likely the result of stress and suggests that more stress exposure training is needed to address this issue. In the non-lethal scenarios, an insufficient reactionary gap (placing themselves too close to the suspects prior to employing their first force option) was the most common tactical error that hindered performance.

Initial Threat Response Training Implications

Effective threat engagement requires sound decisions that are based upon situation awareness and threat identification. The context of the situation combined with the officer's ability should guide the response strategy. Without repeated exposure to similar situations (previous experience), individuals typically fail to solve the problem correctly. Often students base their threat response decisions on their most recent training or something they read that dealt with a similar situation, rather than critically analyzing the situation and figuring out the best technique. To improve threat response scores, training should expose students to dynamic rapidly evolving scenarios that require the student to make decisions on both lethal and non-lethal threat responses. The scenarios should illustrate the dangers of unsound decisions for threat response, and using Student-Centered Feedback, develop strategies and skills that lead to decisions that are more effective.

Scene Control Observations

Figure 2-8 shows the ratings for "Scene Control" (after initial engagement) which produced the lowest composite scenario score compared to the other STAR factors as shown in Figure 2-3. With the exception of rendering aid to the injured, students had difficulty controlling the scene once initial engagement was made. Once the immediate threats are controlled, the officer's next responsibility is to prevent individuals from altering or destroying physical evidence. Officers should restrict the uncontrolled movements of victims, witnesses, and suspects while ensuring and maintaining safety at the scene.

Scene Control Training Implications

During the scenarios, student's demonstrated difficulty transitioning from the active engagement portion to controlling the scene. The score "Not Acceptable" was the most prevalent rating received in all four scenarios; likely the result of limited exposure to threat prioritization situations and abbreviated scenarios—where "out of role" is called too soon after the initial

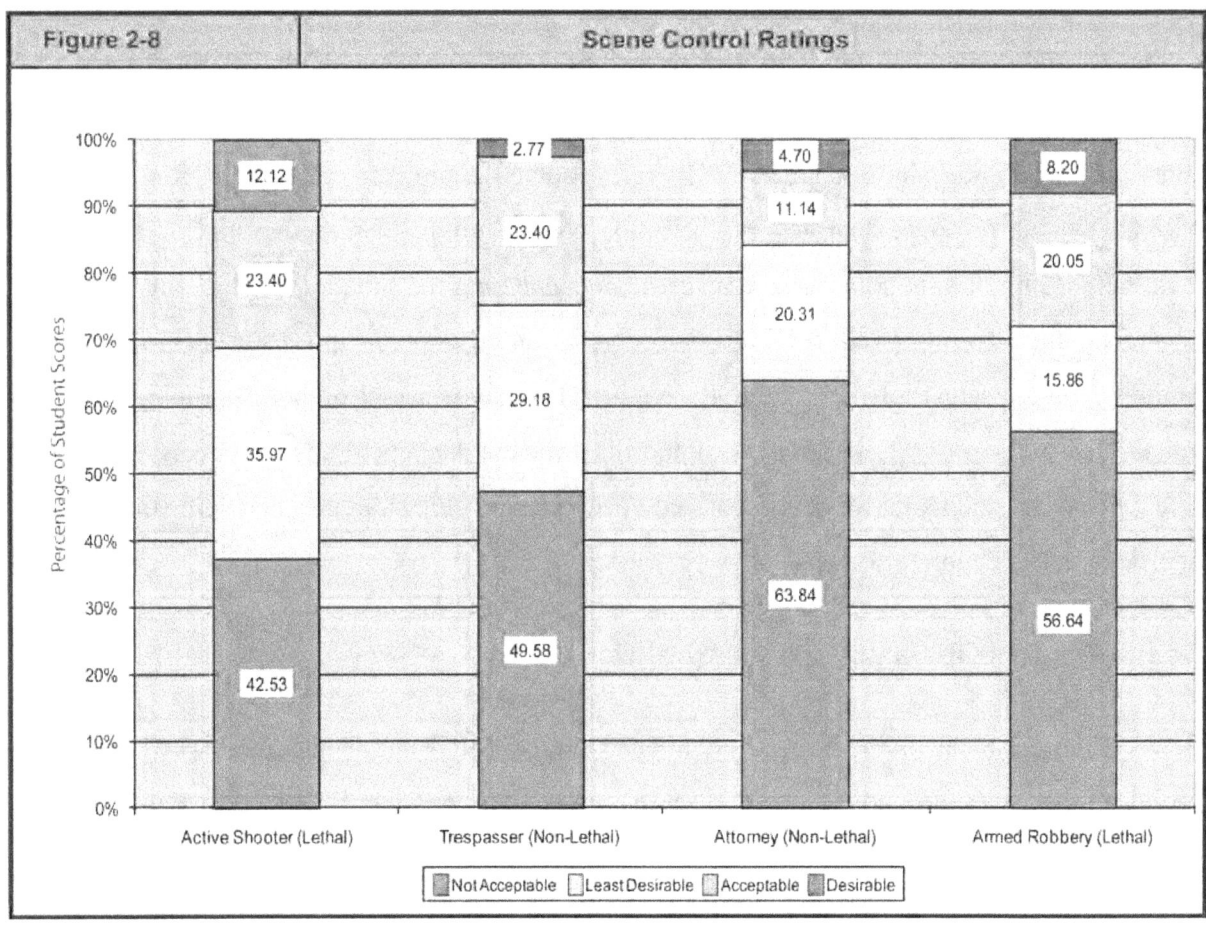

threat is controlled. When subsequent actions are not performed, students are left with incomplete memories for future use and will have difficulty in re-orienting (OODA Loop) as they transition to the next task ahead. The research team recommends providing more scenarios that expose students to multiple-threat and non-threat situations for the development of complete mental models. These scenarios should be created to include the elements of situation awareness, threat identification, threat prioritization, communication, and control of non-immediate threats under stress.

Arrest Techniques Observations

Student "Arrest Techniques" ratings for each scenario are shown in Figure 2-9. Student arrest techniques were stronger for the first two scenarios, "Active Shooter" and "Trespasser,"

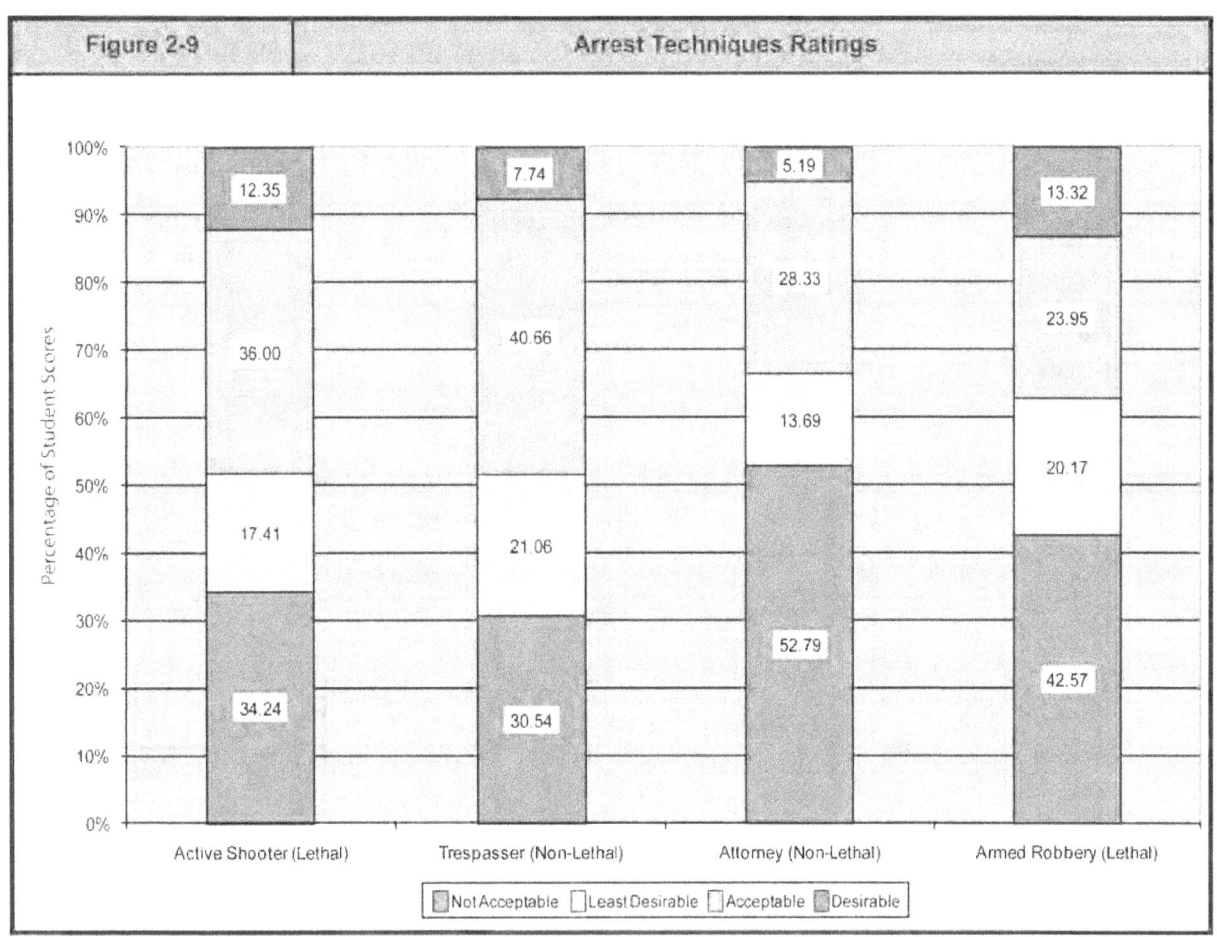

but diminished in the latter two scenarios of "Attorney" and "Armed Robbery." One possible explanation for the drop in performance: Day 2 scenarios utilized an increased number of role-players, making the threat identification process more difficult, which slowed down mental processing of the OODA Loop. Specific issues identified during the arrest techniques process included not searching the suspect, non-systematic pat downs, bouncing between suspects, and failing to locate weapons which are detailed in the appendix.

Arrest Techniques Training Implications

During Scene Control scenarios, students demonstrated difficulty performing arrest procedures and prioritizing their actions. While increased levels of stress, weak situation awareness, and limited threat prioritization contributed to these ratings, the research team felt increased exposure to situations similar to those presented in this study would be of great benefit. The research team surmised that calling "Out of Role" too soon during training scenarios prevents students from developing critical arrest and search skills. The research team suggests that students receive more exposure to resistive suspects and are required to locate items other than weapons during the search incident to arrest.

Application of Force Observations

Figure 2-10 shows the ratings for "Application of Force" (proper force option and technique to threat level) during each scenario. Students demonstrated the greatest level of

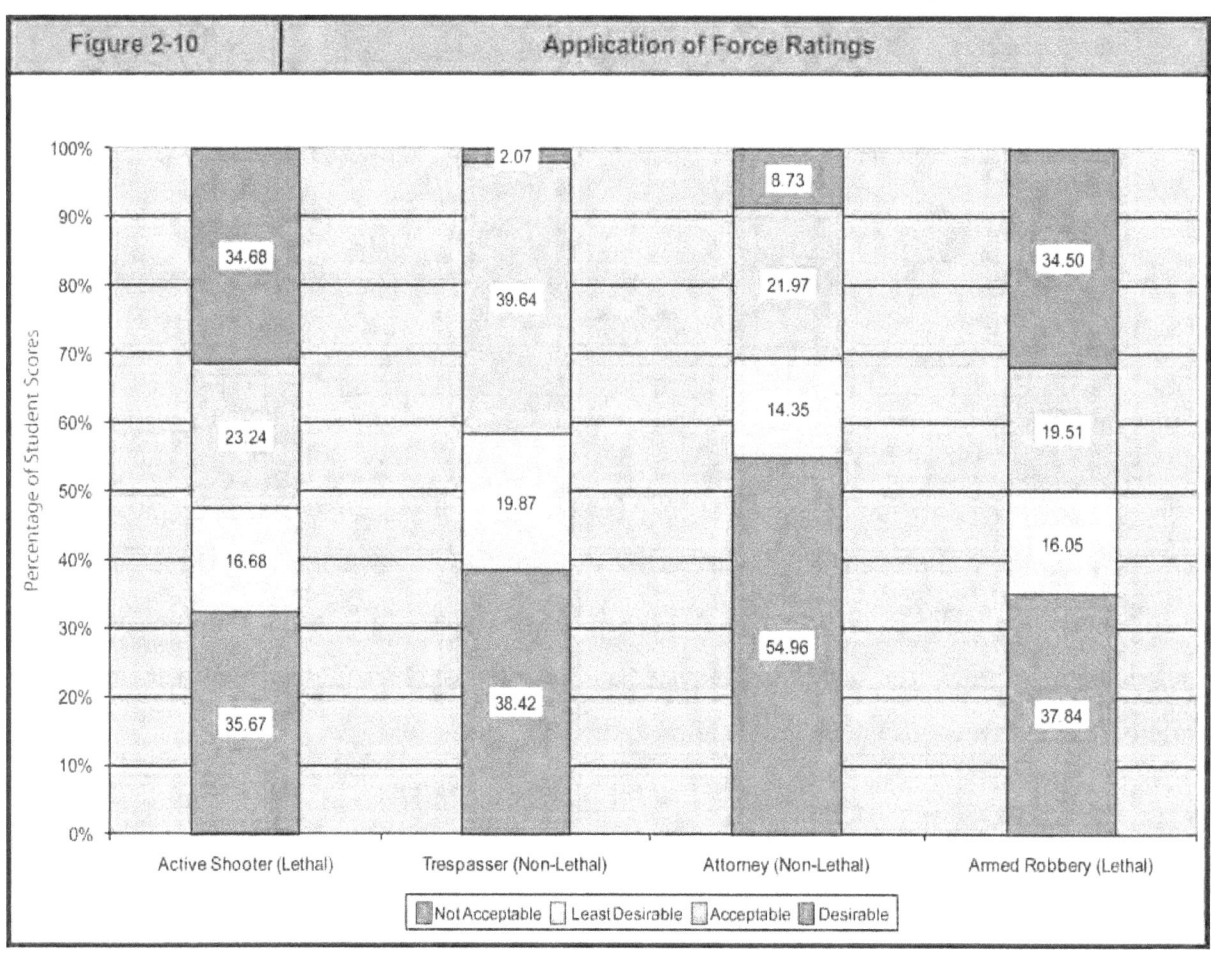

"desirable" responses during the two lethal scenarios. Both lethal scenarios were developed with fact patterns requiring immediate engagement of the threat. The non-lethal scenarios were designed with a component requiring students to recognize that their first force option was not effective, and requires a transition to a second force option to subdue the suspect.

Application of Force Training Implications

The time required for the students to execute a force option suggests difficulty in making use-of-force decisions and in prioritizing their actions. Effective threat engagement requires rapid problem solving skills which come from realistic training. The value of video playback during the feedback sessions was highly effective for the documentation of effective officer actions and response times (Student-Centered Feedback is discussed in detail in Section 4). Due to the distorted perception of time caused by stress, it was only due to the video enhanced feedback that students were able to clearly see what actions were or were not taken, as well as the effectiveness of their actions. The video-assisted feedback allowed both research team and students to quickly focus on the same issues, eliminate any doubt concerning the performance, and more effectively use after-action-review time to improve future performance.

Communication Observations

Figure 2-11 shows student ratings for "Communication" (student does/does not effectively communicate) during each scenario. Student communication skills were varied during the four scenarios, with specific element scores generally being higher for lethal versus non-lethal scenarios. The student's ability to acquire information about suspects was acceptable to desirable during the early segment of each scenario; however, as the events began to unfold, the ability to use communication skills began to diminish. Similarly, presentation of a strong command presence through communication also decreased during the scenario.

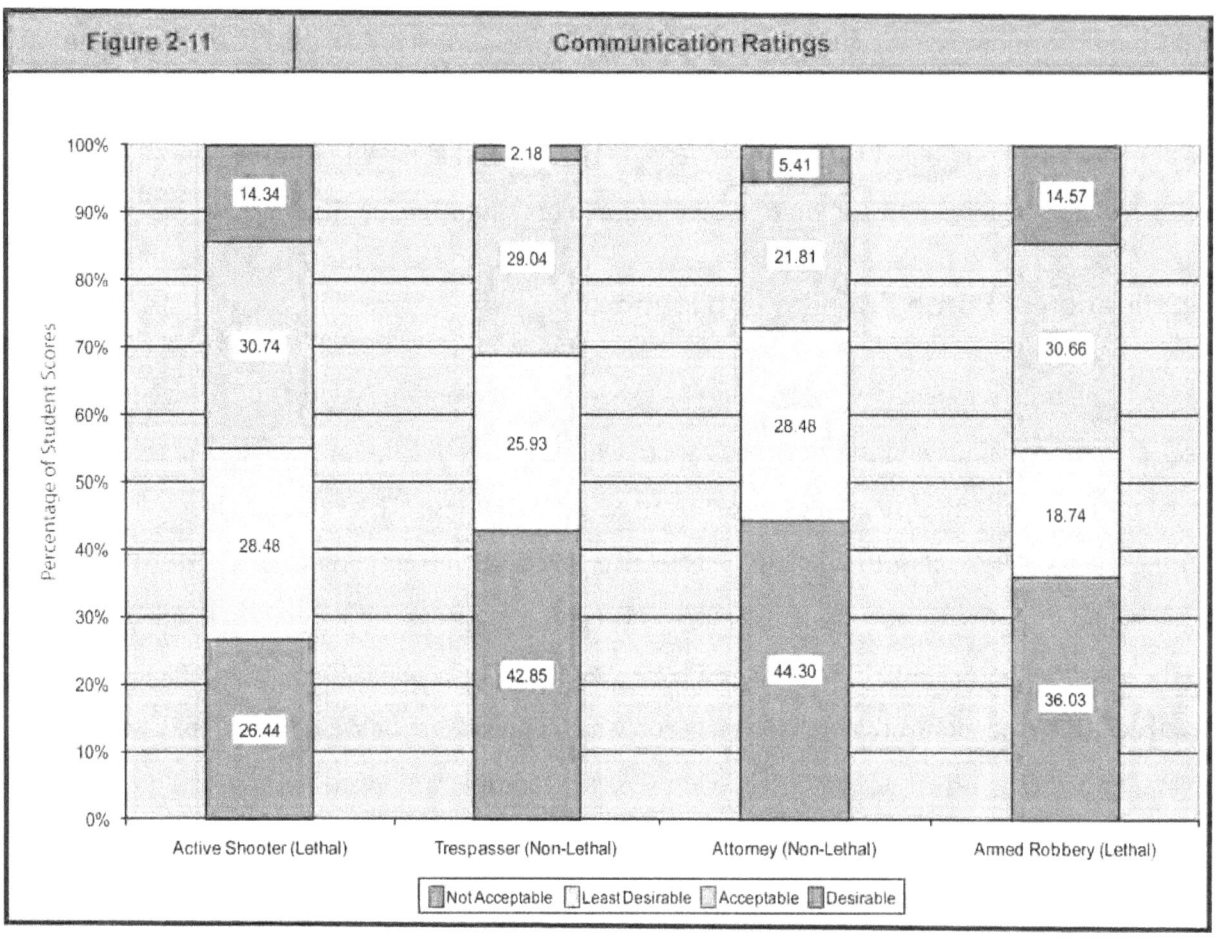

Figure 2-11 — **Communication Ratings**

Communication Training Implications

Stressful situations make communication more difficult. The research team concluded that communication activities need to be routinely inserted into stressful scenarios to ensure that these skills would be employed during a dynamic encounter. The research team also recommends exploring additional ways to integrate this skill into additional training areas. Although a simple task to perform, communication is frequently the first skill forgotten in a stressful encounter; yet, it may be the most critical for survival.

Articulation Observations

Figure 2-12 shows the student ratings for "Articulation" (After Action Review) during each scenario. The student's ability to articulate details and relevant facts after the scenarios completed were encouraging; with more than half the students receiving acceptable or desirable ratings on three of the four scenarios.

Articulation Training Implications

The research team recommends using Student-Centered Feedback and reality-based training scenarios to develop the student's ability to recall details, and articulate both the facts and circumstances associated with use of force.

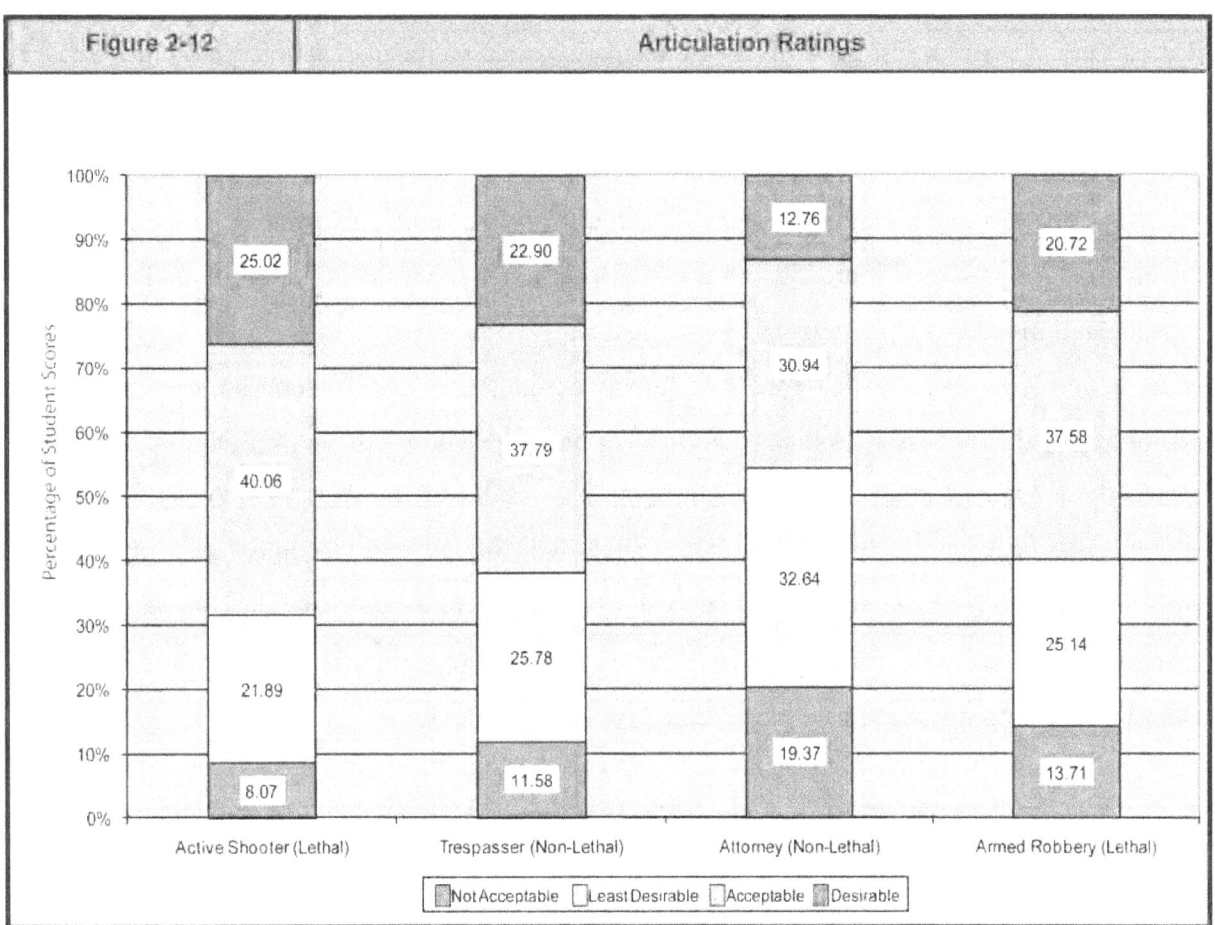

| Figure 2-12 | Articulation Ratings |

Summary

The ability to employ proper tactics requires the ability to make decisions rapidly under stress. This capacity is most critical in situations that quickly escalate, and where life or death may depend on a fast, appropriate response. This research study designed two lethal force (Active Shooter and Armed Robbery), and two non-lethal force (Trespasser and Attorney) scenarios that would challenge students and compel them to draw upon their training. The stressful scenarios were created to realistically model lethal and non-lethal force situations typical for law enforcement officers and agents. This research project also incorporated a new assessment model, the Scenario Training Assessment and Review (STAR). The STAR identifies techniques to evaluate student selection of appropriate responses, and the integration of those responses into performance during stressful, fast-moving, life-like incidents. The STAR provides a process for evaluating highly fluid situations that demand continuous, accurate assessment of effective decisions, and changing tactics.

One of the first summary observations made is that students generally perform their best in situations that most closely replicate the training they received. Although each scenario was new to the participants—and they did not know the "who, what, when, and where" of any scenario—the "Active Shooter" scenario reflected the best overall performance as measured by the eight STAR factors (Figure 2-2). Basic students have been trained to identify and respond to lethal situations as this is recognized as a critical skill within basic training. A comparison of the lethal to non-lethal scenarios (Figure 2-4) quickly demonstrates that students are more adept at responding and controlling a lethal situation as opposed to a non-lethal confrontation. Trainees clearly demonstrated a higher performance level in every STAR factor in the lethal scenarios which is good news for officer safety. Although lethal situations are of critical importance, law enforcement officers must realize that the majority of calls they will respond to are non-lethal. Effectively responding to routine calls will have a major impact on officer survivability by not allowing those events to escalate beyond the level of non-lethal.

The STAR factors provide a unique perspective by identifying eight skills that, when blended together, create scenarios that replicate real-world confrontations. During this research study, the STAR was able to demonstrate a two-fold benefit. First, the STAR demonstrated that as a scoring tool it could measure performance "real-time" and provide prompt feedback at the conclusion of the scenario. This is a challenging requirement as law enforcement skills typically become blurred in a dynamic encounter. Secondly, the STAR factors allow specific skill areas to be isolated for further review and analysis during a video playback. The comparison chart (Figure 2-3) of the STAR factors indicate that students are generally knowledgeable about which tactics to perform (Articulation/AAR, Situation Awareness), but require additional practice to perform the tactics correctly and completely. This is consistent with being stuck in the OODA Loop and not yet having the cognitive processing to transfer the recently learned skills and adapt them for new situations—the concept of "moderate transfer". The factor of "Control" was clearly the weakest area of performance as it contributed the lowest score in each of the four scenarios.

As mentioned previously, students performed their best in the "lethal, single-suspect" scenario. The research team also identified "control" problems with several scenarios, commenting that students would demonstrate a satisfactory response to a threat, but were not always able to complete the arrest. One explanation for the lack of thoroughness: training classes may be calling "out of role" too soon; not providing students with adequate opportunities to perform an arrest to completion.

Providing realistic situations in which trainees can refine their skills is always a challenge. Being able to identify the threat(s) in a crowded environment will continue to be a challenge in both real-life and training environments. Once again, students performed better with the more familiar situation of a single (non-lethal) "Trespasser," and a single (lethal) "Active Shooter" where it was somewhat easier to identify and focus on the threat. This is in contrast to the crowded (non-lethal) "Attorney" and crowded/multiple threat (lethal) "Armed Robbery" scenarios; where threat identification was more complex, and hence, produced slower response times (Appendix 3 / Table 6). Boyd's Loop provides a reminder that students need realistic training and exposure to build memories that will allow, in future situations, to not only Observe and Orient, but more importantly Decide and Act. If there aren't sufficient experiential memories to call upon, individuals will be unable to decide and act effectively.

A final summary statement must be made at this point as to the specificity of training and the non-transfer of training. Based upon the results of this study and previous studies, trainers should not be under the false assumption that training with single suspects will prepare students for dealing with multiple suspects; or that training for lethal situations will prepare students for non-lethal situations. They do not. Students need to participate in a variety of specifically designed situations, performed thoroughly until completion, and in this manner will establish valuable memories for future use. This diversity of training may well prove to be lifesaving.

Recommendations

Recommendation 1

The findings suggest that students require a greater amount of reality-based training if they are to perform successfully in situations comparable to those presented here. Scenarios must expose students to both multiple-threat and non-threat individuals in order for students to develop clear mental models. These experiences help officers/agents develop the necessary skills to execute arrests and maintain officer safety. The scenarios also need to incorporate the elements (STAR factors) of situation awareness, threat prioritization, control of multiple threats, arrest and search techniques, application of force, and communication.

Recommendation 2

Overall, findings suggest that training for nonlethal encounters requires modification. The research team suggests that incorporation of additional use-of-force training scenarios, requiring non-lethal force options other than verbal control—as well as some form of physical control—will lead to more effective training and better prepared graduates. The findings also suggest that instructors are calling "Out of Role" too soon during training scenarios—preventing students from developing critical arrest and search skills.

Recommendation 3

The findings of this report indicate that the STAR assessment model, combined with video-supplemented, Student-Centered Feedback, are ideal tools to enhance training effectiveness and establish accurate mental models (memories)—essential for effective law enforcement responses in dynamic, high-stress encounters such as those presented in this study.

Recommendation 4

The reaction time findings should be reviewed by the appropriate FLETC Training Divisions associated with lethal and nonlethal techniques to determine if the types and response times are satisfactory and, if not, take appropriate steps to address any training deficiency.

Recommendation 5

The findings suggest that students have inadequate communication skills when they need them most—during stressful encounters. The research team recommends an emphasis be placed on proper law enforcement communication during reality-based training scenarios and Student-Centered Feedback. The scenarios need to reinforce interpersonal and radio techniques during challenging encounters in order to develop mental models.

Recommendation 6

The findings suggest that students need additional exposure to resistive suspects, and be required to locate and respond to items, other than weapons, during a search incident to an arrest. The inclusion of additional routine items (keys, cell phone, and wallet) to be found on suspects will provide searches that are more realistic during training, and more effective during performance evaluation.

Intentionally left blank

SECTION III

The Impact of Emotions On Performance

3

The Impact of Emotions on Performance

Introduction

An important component of law enforcement training is determining whether students can perform skills taught not only under routine conditions, but also under stressful conditions. Analysis of data from previous SSRP research indicated deterioration of the decision making process during the high stress scenario. Observations concluded that 70 percent of the test subjects made ineffective tactical decisions; 70 percent displayed an inability to correct equipment malfunctions; and 49 percent failed to maintain a position of advantage during specific phases of the research scenario. Any of these deficiencies could result in serious consequences during a high-risk law enforcement encounter. Additionally, the emotions of anxiety and anger were identified as the two most important emotions affecting performance during the scenario. Being able to think clearly and perform effectively under stress is critical to increase the odds of surviving a deadly force encounter.

In order to evaluate performance under stressful conditions, scenarios must be carefully designed to elicit stress similar to on-the-job encounters, and use validated measures to provide meaningful results. An assessment tool is needed to measure stress levels to determine the impact of stress on decision making, and to guide future training efforts. The Spielberger State Trait Personality Inventory (STPI) and State Trait Anger Expression Inventory (STAXI) were used previously for the SSRP, and were further refined for use in this study (Spielberger, 1979; Spielberger and Reheiser, 2009). The STPI and STAXI values not only provide a basis for measuring the intensity of stress following a research scenario, but can also be used to determine stress levels in future scenarios that require a specific stress level for novices or experts. The research team developed a series of scenarios simulating the demands of law enforcement encounters. By exposing the students to these scenarios and subsequent evaluation, the research team desired to determine whether multiple exposures would reduce emotional stress, thereby improving decision making and performance.

Designing Stress-Evoking Scenarios

Incorporating elements of realism into scenario design is of critical importance in law enforcement training. In order to observe the effects of acute (perceived immediate threat) stress on performance, there must be a "suspension of disbelief" or a mental state where the performer becomes so immersed in the action that the "simulated environment" becomes a "believable, real environment." In order for a scenario to emulate the real world, the scenario should include various elements that have been well documented and add to its realism.

Factors that produce anxiety or stress, known as stressors, can occur in many forms: reduced time to perform (time pressure), increased number of activities to be accomplished (task load), increased anticipation of physical or psychological harm (threat), unwanted sounds (noise), unexpected or uncertain events (novelty), reduced energy (fatigue), and increased consequences for error (performance pressure). A scenario can use a single stressor or any combination of stressors depending on the objectives of the scenario. Simply stated, stress results when an individual's perception of the demands exceeds one's resources. Participating in stressful scenarios contribute to developing skills that become more resilient with practice. By introducing realism and variability in the desired training environment, students are able to improve their future performance and respond more effectively using the tactical responses stored in memory.

Research Design of Scenarios

The research team created four scenarios designed to evoke two different levels of stress: high and low. The research team assumed the two nonlethal scenarios would create low stress levels while the lethal scenarios would result in high stress levels. The scenarios were intended to represent a unique event requiring students to make decisions under varying levels of threat, situation awareness, with escalating time and response pressure. All four scenarios were designed for single officer/agent response to the situation and designed to be winnable; however, each scenario provided numerous opportunities for decisions and possible mistakes. Each mistake could escalate the risk factors associated with the scenario. Selection for the research study was limited to three students from each class in order to ensure that students had no prior knowledge of a scenario's composition. Additionally, all participants were asked to not disclose any details of the scenarios to other students.

The research team identified training requirements, tasks, and competencies, based on research of field incident reports and adjudicated cases. Essential scenario information was documented on a Scenario Worksheet (Appendix 4). Critical incident data and input from SMEs was used to create specific events ("trigger" events or sequences) that were embedded into the scenario. Each event was described in the scenario sequence column of the Scenario Worksheet, the applicable Enabling Performance Objectives (EPOs) and lesson plan title is identified under the Performance Objective column, and expected performance is listed under the Performance Measure column. The expected performance associated with the event reflects the training standard and must be consistent with adjudicated cases. In brief, key events were designed to act as cues that trigger essential actions or behaviors, and provide the basis for evaluation of the students. The key events provide opportunities for performance observation, evaluation, and feedback. The research team used these documents to estimate and adjust scenario stress based on a consensus of scenario difficulty. Scenario difficulty was based on:

1. Amount of information provided to the student about and during the situation;
2. Number and type of immediate threats incorporated into the scenario;
3. Number and type of secondary threats and when they occur;
4. Force options required to control the immediate and secondary threats;
5. Number of victims and witnesses that must be controlled during the scenario; and
6. Resources (backup, visibility, etc.) available to the student during the scenario.

In the framework of the research design, it was presumed that the student's ability to assess the situation and respond would be guided by the level of risk involved. For example, a moving violation traffic stop—presumably less than lethal force contact—is thought to be lower risk, and therefore lower stress; while a felony vehicle stop—potential lethal force contact—is believed to be a high-risk, higher stress training scenario. The research team ranked the scenarios in the following order: the two nonlethal scenarios were expected to be the least difficult out of the four, with the Trespasser scenario ranked least stressful; and the two lethal scenarios were considered more difficult than the nonlethal scenarios, with the Armed Robbery scenario being the most difficult (and most stressful). While the research team made every attempt to design the scenarios for a specific level of stress, the nonlethal scenarios did not provide a performance environment that evoked lower levels of stress. It is presumed that this is not an isolated situation; as pre-determining levels of difficulty and stress is a common challenge for law enforcement trainers. This challenge identifies the need for a more accurate process to evaluate scenarios—a process that incorporates the student's perspective to ensure that a scenario will accomplish its desired goals. The tools used to measure emotional stress in this study were the Spielberger State Trait Personality Inventory (STPI) and State Trait Anger Expression Inventory (STAXI).

Assessing Stress Emotions

The Spielberger State Trait Personality Inventory (STPI) and State Trait Anger Expression Inventory (STAXI) were used to evaluate student perception of stress. The Spielberger instrument was selected due to the reliability and validity of the self-report items under both research and clinical environments (Spielberger and Reheiser, 2004; Spielberger, Ritterland, Sydeman, Reheiser and Unger, 1995). STPI and STAXI values were used to measure the type and amount of emotion that was aroused during the scenario by comparing pre- and post-performance measures.

Stress causes emotional reactions such as anxiety (feeling of nervousness, apprehension, fear, or worry) and anger (feeling of frustration, aggression, guilt, or revenge). The degree to which students perceive a given stimulus as threatening or difficult dictates its effect on "state" emotions (the temporary intensity of feelings), and "trait" emotions the (general tendency to routinely respond to a specific stressor). The interpretation of a situation, as a present or anticipated danger, will vary the intensity of anxiety and anger. The elevation of State-Anxiety and Anger scores also can be triggered by recall of traumatic events similar to the current situation. The intensity and frequency of State-Anxiety scores can be increased if the individual has high Trait-Anxiety. Spielberger also identified that individuals who tend to suppress their anger also tend to experience anxiety more often, and those with anger scores above the 75th percentile tend to experience feelings that interfere with optimal performance.

The emotions measured on the STPI/STAXI instrument are briefly defined in Appendix 5, Table 1. In addition to the primary emotion scales (Anxiety and Anger), the customized instrument also collected data on Curiosity (inquisitive interest), Depression (self-deprecating thoughts), eight anger sub-scales, and a general anger expression score. The customized assessment instrument provided instructions for self-rating on the intensity and frequency of the individual STPI/STAXI items. During the baseline administration, both trait and state items were given, with instructions to rate the extent that each item is currently or generally experienced. The post-scenario instrument included only the state items with instructions to respond to the items from the perspective of while they were engaged in the scenario. This procedure was repeated at the end of each scenario to determine the emotional levels experienced during the scenario.

State Anxiety and State Anger Scores

The STPI/STAXI scores in Figure 3-1 identify the perceived stress levels prior to the research (baseline), and following each scenario. Both State Anxiety and State Anger had statistically significant increases during each of the four scenarios when compared to baseline values. In comparison, the average (reference) State Anxiety percentile score for normal adult females is 58, and 52 for adult males. For neuropsychiatric patients, a reaction characterized by abnormal apprehension or uneasiness, the average State Anxiety percentile score is 88. Symptoms of acute anxiety include a reaction of intense fear, horror, or helplessness. The average SSRP State Anxiety percentile score ranged from a low of 50.56 to a high of 87.39. The reported State Anxiety levels associated with each scenario is sufficient to disrupt normal physical and psychological functioning.

The reference State Anger percentile scores are 60 and 70 for normal adult females and males, respectively, with scores between 25 and 75 falling within the normal range. Individuals with higher anger scores are more prone to experience adverse effects on decisions and performance than those with lower scores. The "Attorney" scenario generated the highest State Anger value of 84.79. The reported state anger scores in the four scenarios were sufficient to

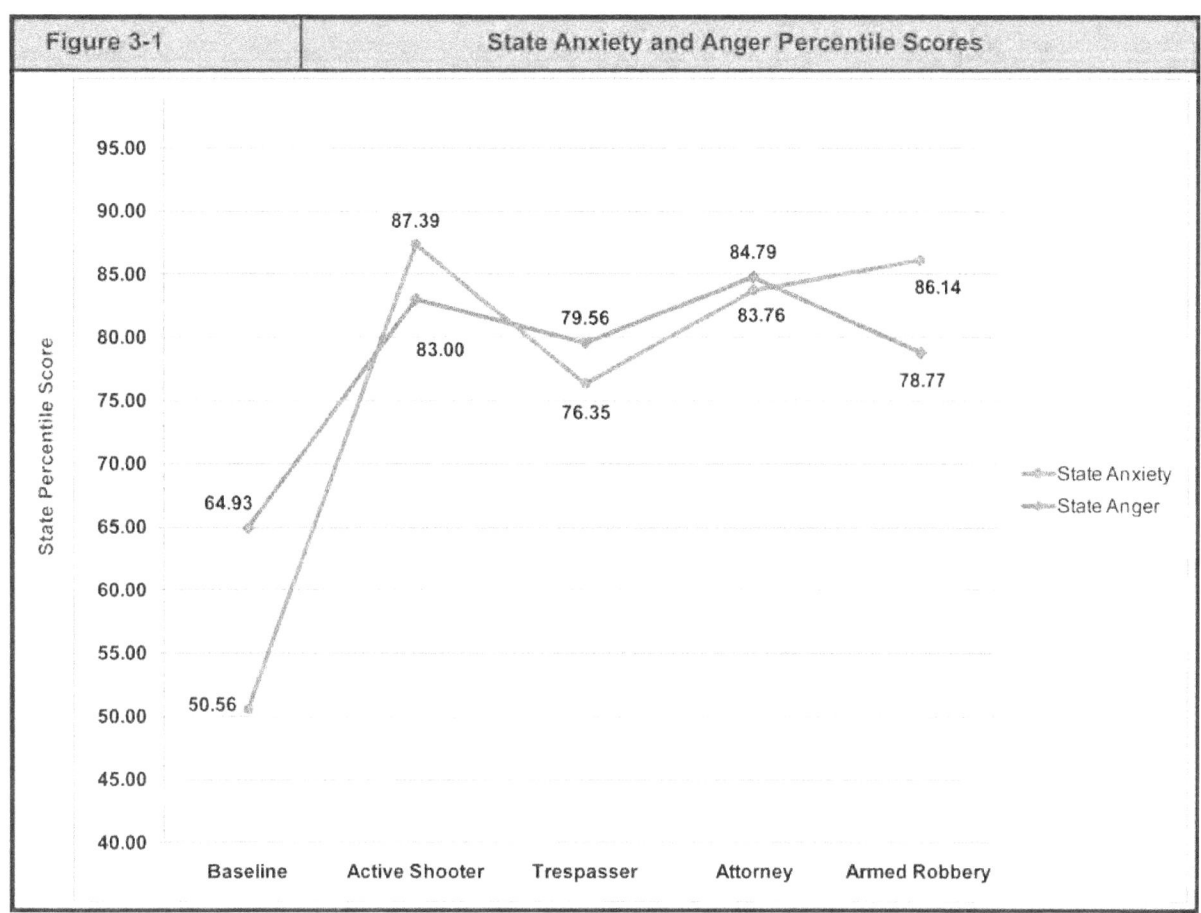

Figure 3-1

activate the autonomic nervous system to a degree that would result in intense angry feelings. Individuals experiencing anger at this level tend to express it in verbally or physically aggressive behavior. Both verbal and physical expressions of anger were observed during the scenarios.

Scenario Stress Index

A second measure was used to determine a combined or overall stress score for each of the four scenarios. Using Spielberger's guidelines, the scores for State Anxiety and Anger were combined and normalized by controlling for each student's trait score (this step provided a stress baseline value used for comparisons). The combination of Anger and Anxiety Values produced a "perceived stress score" and allows for a comparison of stress levels between the four scenarios (Figure 3-2). Using this procedure, the "Attorney" scenario was the most stressful with an overall score of 73.65. This was most surprising and unexpected—that a nonlethal scenario would create more stress than either of the lethal scenarios. The research team had anticipated

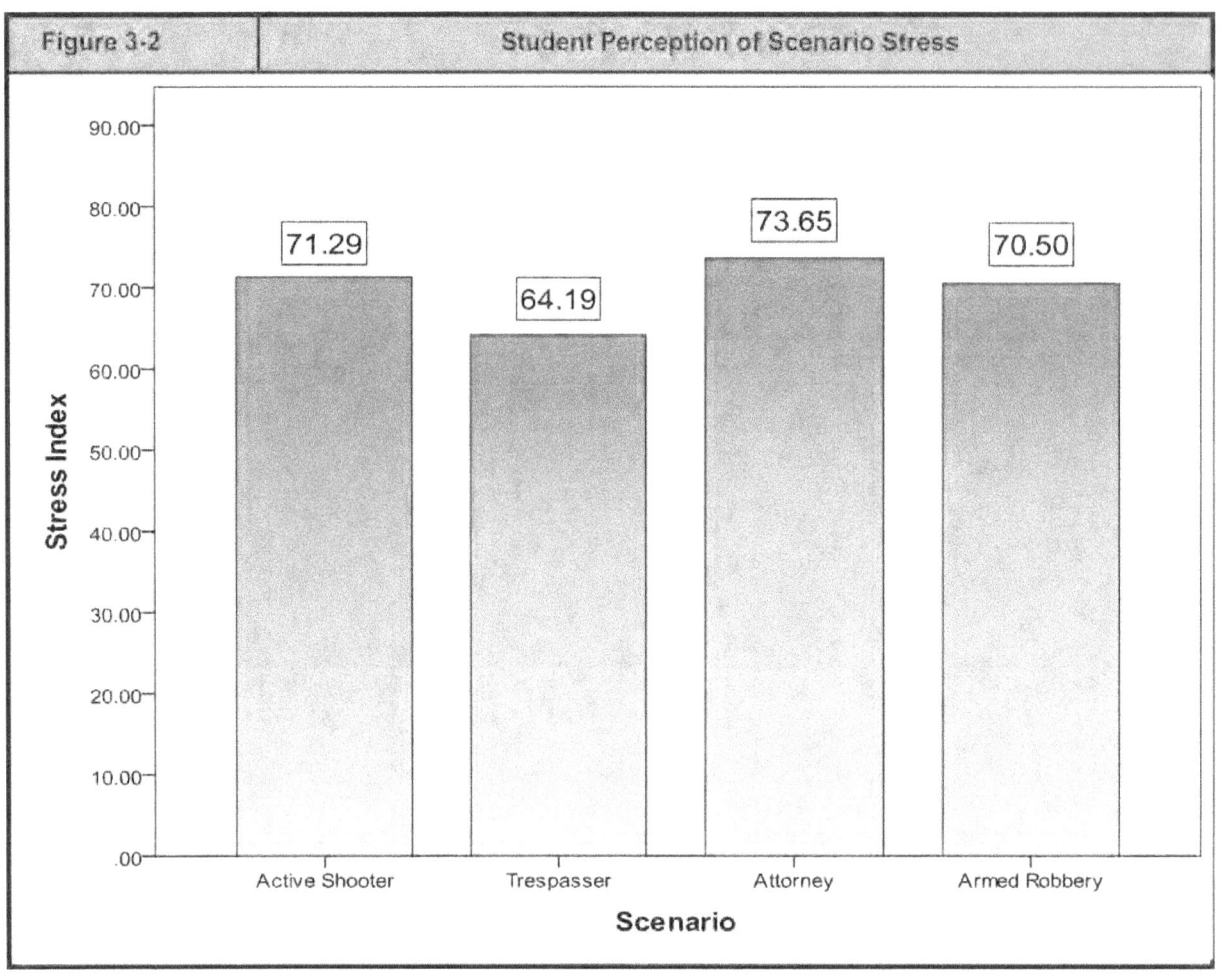

| Figure 3-2 | Student Perception of Scenario Stress |

just the opposite. Although numerical differences are shown in Figure 3-2, the differences between the two lethal and the two nonlethal scenarios are not statistically significant.

Figure 3-2 also serves to reinforce the concept that stress is determined by the performer, and although the scenarios were designed by experienced trainers, only the students themselves could determine how prepared (or unprepared) they were to perform as law enforcement officers. The Scenario Stress Index provides a mechanism for which scenario stress levels can be scored, compared, and classified for future use in training.

Emotions and Performance Scores

One research question, asked during scenario development, was whether exposure to four stressful encounters would begin to show a "stress inoculation" pattern—where the stress response would be noticeably reduced. To determine if there was a reduced stress response, statistical procedures were used to compare performance scores and STPI/STAXI scores. A decrease in the number of significant relationships during the last three scenarios suggests that students were adjusting to the "testing effect" of performing under testing conditions.

The effects of anxiety and anger were more prominent during the two lethal scenarios. Low and moderate levels of State Anxiety enhanced performance scores until, as described earlier, the scores passed the 60th percentile mark—where too much anxiety caused performance to diminish. High levels of State Anger also had a negative impact on performance scores. An interesting occurrence took place during the "nonlethal" scenarios with regard to stress. Rather than observing a moderate range of high-to-low anger and anxiety scores (as in the "lethal" scenarios), the emotions were all similarly high. This suggests that the students were all equally stressed, and had no mental models to call upon for the challenges associated with the "nonlethal" scenarios. The performance scores also suggest that the students were more mentally prepared for the lethal scenarios than the nonlethal scenarios.

An additional pattern was observed—the impact of State Anger on performance. State Anger and two of its sub-scales (Feeling and Verbal) are the most significant state emotion variables associated with poor performance. As indicated by Spielberger, there is a distinctive change in performance at the 60—75th percentile. Once individuals cross a threshold of anger, performance deteriorates rapidly (Spielberger and Reheiser 2009).

Important Elements for Scenario Design

A primary goal for most training scenarios is to provide a realistic environment that allows students to demonstrate their knowledge, skills, and abilities. For the scenario experience to be a meaningful, memory enhancing experience, the scenario should reflect situations that will likely occur again in the future. Real situations commonly include a starting point or trigger event, tasks or challenges, and a conclusion. In order for scenarios to replicate this sequence, they should have a logical beginning, that in some manner introduces students to the situation (dispatched, patrol, or spontaneous); allows them to identify and resolve the primary tasks (control of suspects, witnesses, and appropriate management of victims, scene safety); and perform those activities necessary to bring the scenario to a natural conclusion. This also infers that, since scenario training time is typically limited due to time- and role-player constraints, using situations that officers rarely/never encounter is counterproductive to making students street-ready (Murray, 2004). To summarize, scenario design should follow the general format; provide a realistic beginning; contain a primary task or challenge; and conclude as realistically and completely as it would on the job.

- **Logical Beginning**
- **Uncertain Challenge**
- **Thorough Finish**
- **Over-arching Components**

Logical Beginning

In order to prepare students for real-world encounters, scenarios should be designed to use realistic cues and trigger events that would prompt the brain to recall the practiced mental model(s) in future situations. One strategy for providing a natural beginning or lead-in for a scenario is to provide the information in the scenario briefing. This step will provide a realistic transition as to "why or how" students would be responding to that particular situation. Through the addition of realistic cues, the training scenarios seem more "job-like" for students, and trainers are provided with more opportunities to observe the totality of the student's decisions and ramifications of the decisions. When scenarios are too short, students have fewer opportunities to demonstrate competency or explain their thought process to the trainer. Scenarios should begin in a typical manner (such as a call from dispatch) to give trainers an opportunity to observe the student's ability to assess and respond to the situation. When trainers conclude scenarios too early or verbally telling the student to skip a step (such as a search) to observe another skill, it limits training opportunities or/and leads to a false sense of competence in the trainee. If it is not observed, it cannot be evaluated; and if it is not evaluated, competence cannot be determined.

Uncertain Challenge

Adding uncertainty to scenarios trains the brain to become accustomed to increased stimuli—enhancing attentiveness and cue recognition, and forming motor responses that are linked to the stimuli. Uncertainty in scenario design means the student does not know what is going to occur. For example, whenever students are dressed out in FX safety gear, the scenario should not always be a shoot situation. Predictable scenarios limit the development of decision making skills, and opportunities for trainers to determine whether students possess shoot/no-shoot decision making ability. Uncertainty does not mean that role players take it upon themselves to deviate from the scenario's role-player script or lesson plan. The purpose of uncertainty is to provide novel and challenging experiences for students, as well as opportunities for skill assessment. This means the scenario must be a novel encounter for the twentieth student as well as the first. Uncertainty in scenarios includes conditions of task ambiguity, where students may face doubts regarding the nature of the task situation, available alternatives, and possible outcomes related to these alternatives. These scenarios include task environments that are more dynamic, in which unexpected events occur suddenly and require adjustment to adapt to varying situational requirements. This uncertain paradigm leads to changes in behavior because students must adapt their actions to match the changing situation. Uncertainty challenges students to develop their situation awareness, cue recognition, and decision skills because they do not have foreknowledge of when or where the threat may occur, the speed with which conditions may change. In addition, incorporating uncertain challenges like weapon failures, bystanders with cameras, unfriendly crowds, and other realistic distractions is reflective of real-world encounters. Students, trained to focus their attention on the critical aspects of a task, are better able to prioritize their options, and select the response that provides the best outcome.

Once students have reached the point where they are familiar with the basic skills, it is time to increase the variety of situations which will challenge decision making skills presented in class. Training scenarios should require students to apply lethal, less than lethal, and verbal control techniques (Murray, 2004). Not every law enforcement encounter ends up in a shoot situation; not all training scenarios should either. Students need to practice their control techniques on suspects with varying degrees of cooperation. Students need to be challenged with making shoot/don't shoot, hand control/OC spray, and arrest/don't arrest decisions. Arrest situations are often dynamic, and students need to understand that, although many cues may indicate that a situation is "low risk," it only takes a moment for the risk to escalate dramatically.

Thorough Finish

Scenario designs that allow students to proceed to a natural conclusion are critical to reinforce proper tactics and control of the crime scene (Bostain, 2006). FBI reports (Federal Bureau of Investigation, 2006) that it is during the post-incident control of suspects, witnesses, and victims that officers overlook critical elements. Typical errors include improper handcuffing, searches, and securing the scene to protect evidence and make it safe for other personnel. The FBI report reveals that 38 percent of all U.S. officers killed were affecting an arrest, with 60 percent of these officers acting alone. Observations during the SSRP indicated that students could correctly articulate what should be done to control the scene, but were unable to demonstrate the skills required to render the scene safe.

The outcome of the scenario should depend on how students respond to the visual and auditory cues provided in the scenario. Therefore, when students make the correct decisions and limit the suspect's behavior, the scenario could end quickly and without violence. If students fail to respond appropriately to the cues, then the problem should escalate. As in the real world, poor decisions often have serious consequences like those identified in *Violent Encounters* (Federal Bureau of Investigation, 2006). On the other hand, good decisions should be recognized with successful scenario outcomes. Having the scenario outcome predicated by the student's response to scenario cues establishes memory patterns critical to motor program development. This also makes the scenario more realistic.

Over-Arching Components

- **Equipment Fidelity**
- **Sensory Fidelity**
- **Psychological Fidelity**
- **Contextual Environment**

To encourage suspension of disbelief and create the desired level of stress, scenario developers also need to address the component of fidelity in order for scenarios to be realistic and believable. Scenario fidelity is how accurately the scenario reflects realistic conditions.

There are several considerations key to the design of effective scenarios. Because scenarios are a simulation of reality, they should feel "authentic" to the performer. The scenario designer must make decisions as to what real-world features must be included to provide authentic situations, yet, ensure safety of students and role-players. The primary goal is this: after students complete training on how to handcuff a suspect at a vehicle stop, the students should form accurate mental models which will enable them to perform handcuffing effectively at a "real" vehicle stop with minimal apprehension. Scenario fidelity can be categorized into three dimensions: equipment, sensory, and psychological.

Equipment Fidelity

"Equipment fidelity" deals with the degree to which the gear duplicates the appearance and feel of the real equipment used in the field. The use of firearms with live ammunition during a force-on-force scenario would achieve high equipment fidelity but for obvious safety reasons would never be used. On the other end of the spectrum, the use of a rubber "safe" gun during a force-on-force scenario is the safest but it provides a low amount of fidelity. A "blank fire" weapon is an improvement in fidelity with a "FX" marking weapon providing a higher level of fidelity. However, as fidelity is increased, so is the risk. This means that scenario designers must incorporate additional safety precautions. Additional safety precautions, like FX marking round safety gear can have an adverse effect on sensory and psychological fidelity. Compromising equipment fidelity can have unintentional consequences. Observations during the SSRP indicated that 66 percent of the students demonstrated weakness in communication skills when requesting backup and other verbal communication. More specifically, 21 percent did not identify themselves when requesting backup and medical assistance, or failed to press the microphone button when making the call. This adverse behavior may be explained because correct radio procedures could not be practiced during training (low equipment fidelity), stress (all mental activity is focused on the threat) or other possible factors. The important point to understand is that officers need clear mental models for stressful encounters, so that when faced with a stressful event, the lifesaving actions will be performed correctly.

Sensory Fidelity

"Sensory fidelity" is the extent that the simulation duplicates motion cues, visual cues, and other sensory information from the task environment. Sensory components include visual, auditory, and olfactory stimuli, people, movement, and any other cues that prepare the individual for performing the desired task in its natural environment. A primary consideration during the design of a scenario is identification of the amount of stress created by sensory components. A scenario could be defined as high or low in sensory fidelity depending on how well the role-players' motion and visual cues (such as pre-assault indicators) represent realistic situations and behaviors. For example, a scenario that incorporates a role-player portraying a resisting and "struggling" suspect in a busy restaurant where the student must arrest and handcuff the suspect is higher in sensory fidelity than having students handcuff each other in a matted room. Creating training scenarios that have high sensory fidelity requires incorporating the contextual environment where the real task will be performed. This degree of fidelity is essential for effective skill development and enhanced decision making during stressful encounters (Schmidt and Wrisberg, 2008). When training does not provide sensory fidelity, students may be unable to call upon their training when placed in similar, real world environments.

Psychological Fidelity

"Psychological fidelity" is the degree to which students perceive the scenario to be a believable substitute for the target task and environment they could experience on the job. This is a critical factor for law enforcement scenarios as the realism or fidelity of the scenario is based upon the perspective of the student – not the instructor. Ideally, scenario fidelity provides a matching emotional state between the scenario performance and real encounter. A scenario is high in psychological fidelity when students suspend disbelief and interact as they would in an actual law enforcement encounter. Although the three fidelity dimensions are inter-related, suspension of disbelief is the most essential requirement to induce stress during training (Jentsch and Cannon-Bowers, 1998). Without suspending disbelief, students are unlikely to experience stress levels similar to an actual encounter. Documenting and tracking the multidimensional elements of stress, contextual environment, comprehensive scenarios, and fidelity enable scenario designers to be more effective in creating stress-evoking scenarios that achieve the desired training outcomes.

Contextual Environment

Establishing the proper *contextual environment* (conditions associated with an actual event) is critical for scenario development. For example, when testing students by using a "non-compliant" role-player in the middle of a busy restaurant where the student must arrest and handcuff a suspect, because the environment realistically emulates the context of actual arrest events with realistic risks. Practicing handcuffing on classmates in a matted room is essential skill training, but by itself, does not provide the contextual linkage to performance in the real world. The proper contextual environment is critical for developing mental models associated with those memories and proper responses (controlled, rapid, discrete movements). This does not mean that handcuffing in matted rooms should be eliminated from training; but it does mean that training must introduce students to elements like situation awareness, threat identification, and require performance in a high context environment. This also means that testing should be conducted using the proper contextual environment. During the learning of complex skills, the absence or presence of the appropriate contextual environment greatly influences how effectively behaviors are remembered for future use on the job (Clark, 2008).

In the area of firearms training, shooting a qualifying score in a training environment provides a high context (relationship) to other marksmanship activities, but would have a low transfer to the context of engaging an active shooter in the real world. The environmental components in these two examples are significantly different. Although both environments can evoke high levels of stress, anxiety, and fear of failure, each will generate different emotions and thought patterns because of the numerous elements that are different between the two. During qualification shooting, the environment (the range) is likely to be very familiar to the shooter and the events (firing positions) are predetermined and sequential; allowing the mind to focus solely on shooting technique and block out other distractions. Qualification would be described as a near-transfer skill. In contrast, the act of engaging an active shooter would significantly divide the brain's attention between monitoring the actions of the shooter, planning tactics for the officer's response, and scanning the environment for critical cues for threats and opportunities that are likely to be constantly evolving. The brain's operational ability would be further divided by prioritization and contingency planning, and communicating with a partner, team, or dispatch. All this cognitive processing would be taking place while suppressing emotions such as fear of serious injury or death. This situation would require moderate-transfer or far-transfer skills. Although shooting a qualification score is an essential firearm skill, it lacks the uncertainty and adaptability of a realistic, life-or-death, armed confrontation. Training that provides a well-matched contextual environment prepares individuals to feel as if they have faced the situation before and are prepared to respond accordingly in the real world. Scenario designs that incorporate realistic contextual elements enable students to attend to critical cues, improve decision skills, and ability to respond with the correct motor program. Failure to train the brain and its processing ability under conditions that match the contextual environment (the real world environment) can lead to indecision and result in the individual being stuck in the orientation phase of the OODA Loop.

Stress Exposure Training (SET)

Stress Exposure Training (SET), also referred to as "stress inoculation training", is a training technique designed to expose individuals to varying levels of stress to reduce the impact of emotions during subsequent stressful encounters (Meichenbaum, 2003 and Driskell, Salas, Johnston, and Wollert, 2008). SET includes awareness training in psychological factors associated with stress, skill development in making decisions under threat conditions, and implementing those decisions to control situations. The purpose of SET is to develop student confidence and competence in preparation for a realistic stressful encounter. If stress-related emotions cannot be controlled, top-level performance is nearly impossible. The original development of SET was intended for the treatment of patients with phobias, such as inordinate fear of spiders, but has since been modified by the military to enhance performance and hardiness of military personnel in combat. SET incorporates simulation-based training as an interactive, practice-based instructional strategy that provides opportunities for trainees to develop competency and enhance their expertise through scenarios and feedback (Fowlkes, Dwyer, Oser, and Salas, 1998). A complete SET program has three phases: Phase 1 provides information on common reactions to specific stressors; Phase 2 focuses on stress coping skills using practice and feedback; and Phase 3 involves applying stress coping skills under different levels of stress during realistic training scenarios. Benefits of SET include reduced anxiety, increased efficacy, improved performance skills, and improved cognitive and psychomotor performance under stress (Johnston and Cannon-Bowers, 1996). Although there was no formalized SET used in this study, the stress measurement scales were refined in this study with the intention of using the scales for future research in the area of stress and performance.

Mental Models and Stress Exposure

Although there have been many relationships mentioned between emotion scores and scenario performance scores, some relationships have not yet been addressed. Students who experienced only moderate elevations in stress had performance levels similar to those who demonstrated high emotional stress. Dr. Ruth Clark (2008) in her book *Building Expertise* suggests that individuals unable to perform under the conditions associated with the job may be experiencing *transfer failure*. According to Clark, in order for training to transfer, the retrieval of mental models from long term memory into working memory must occur. She goes on to say that the transfer of trained skills requires observing models or examples of correct behavior and then practicing those behaviors in environments similar to those encountered on the job. However, developing effective mental models that transfer learning requires more than a single set of contextual cues. Mental models of correct behavior also require multiple practice exercises designed to challenge students to respond in different ways based on subtle situational changes. This creates flexible mental memories that will accommodate the myriad of unique situations encountered on the job.

Dr. Alexis Artwohl and Loren Christensen (experts on the effects of officer-involved shootings) in their book Deadly Force Encounters offers another insight on training:

> *Most participants in a traumatic event give little or no thought to their behavior; they just instinctively do what their experience has programmed them to do. The more realistic your training is, the more effective it's going to be. With deadly force encounters, realistic training needs to include two basic elements: dynamism, and enough stress to induce a high arousal state. Repetition of deadly force training will help you automatically choose the most effective behavior under the conditions and high arousal stases that characterize most deadly force encounters.* (Artwohl and Christensen, 1997. p. 71)

Artwohl and Christensen are suggesting that successful performance during a traumatic event requires developing some behaviors to the point of automaticity. In other words, individuals that have developed flexible mental models are able to perform better under adverse conditions than individuals that have not. This was observed during the SSRP. For example, individuals that developed effective weapon handling skills were able to rapidly recognize conditions requiring an immediate action procedure, clearing the malfunction, and staying in the fight. These same individuals also had limited recall of the malfunction.

Summary

The law enforcement community has relied on the axiom "Train the way you fight and you will fight the way you train." In order to accomplish this, training must develop skills in an environment that replicates fight conditions and emotions. One of the greatest challenges faced by trainers is creating scenarios that induce the level of stress desired to meet the training objective. Controlling the level of scenario stress is crucial when transitioning students from simple to complex scenarios and building decision making skills using the SET process. This study used a research team of SMEs to create four stressful scenarios and classify them as either high stress or low stress, and then placed them in a specific sequence to measure order effect. Although the intent was that the two nonlethal scenarios would be low stress, and the two lethal scenarios would be high stress, that was not the end result. Because the scenarios did not demonstrate a significant difference in stress levels elicited, it was impossible to test for order effect.

A new variation of the Spielberger STPI/STAXI (the Scenario Stress Index) was used to measure levels of perceived stress. Significant increases in state anxiety and state anger (Figure 3-1), suggests that the scenarios presented the students with a realistic, threatening environment that was stressful. The Scenario Stress Index (Figure 3-2) also indicated that using SMEs to speculate on the level of stress produced by a specific scenario was not an accurate procedure.

It is believed that the SMEs misjudged the level of stress associated with the scenarios because of the difference in perception between SMEs and students. The SMEs have a different and more developed degree of expertise resulting in different perceptions of threat and response than the students. It is extremely difficult to speculate how someone will perceive the magnitude of a threat. A method to measure perceived stress would make this task less daunting. The

Spielberger STPI/STAXI emotion instrument was found to be a more reliable assessment of perceived stress.

The study identified distinct relationships between emotion and performance. When emotion/stress levels are high – performance levels are low; conversely, higher performance scores are observed in those with emotions under control. The best way to summarize this relationship is through a statement made at the 2007 Peaksports Boot Camp by Dr. Ken Ravizza, professor of Applied Sport Psychology at the California State University at Fullerton, and leading authority on stress management skills (Ravizza, 2007), "You must control your emotions before you can control your performance."

Much of the current research has anxiety (fear) as the focal point affecting decision making, and ultimately, performance. While anxiety scores impacted performance during the SSRP scenarios, the study found that anger scores exceeding the 60th percentile had a greater influence negatively impacting performance. This was likely due to the student's perception of lack of control as opposed to fear or threat of personal injury from the suspect. An effective moderator to the effects of acute stress is Stress Exposure Training (SET). Through SET, individuals are forced to perform targeted, progressive activities and make decisions under simulated stressors. The results of SET enhance the ability to recognize the various stressors, provide strategies to mitigate the effects of the stressors, contribute to task over-learning, and increases confidence (Driskell and Johnston, 1998).

In order for law enforcement training to result in desirable graduate performance under stress requires a review of training strategies to ensure that training programs include the "how" and "why" of curriculum design so that it supports the content of "what" we teach. Clark (2008) indicates that training fails to transfer when the skills are developed out of the contextual environments of those found on the job. She also indicates that many organizations are more concerned with learner satisfaction ratings than effectively measured training outcomes. Another concern Clark raises is that most training is directed towards near-transfer performance. This type of training is focused on routine tasks with clear cut decisions and supervisory oversight. There is limited judgment associated with near-transfer tasks. While law enforcement professionals are required to perform near-transfer tasks, field-related survival skills are far-transfer and require the individual to solve problems and exercise judgment in novel and dynamic situations. Successful far-transfer training requires attending to contextual environments and the use of inductive training techniques. Inductive training or student-centered learning encompasses problem-based learning, project-based learning, case-based teaching, discovery learning, and just-in-time teaching (Prince and Felder, 2007).

Recommendations

Recommendation 1

The research team suggests the STPI/STAXI instrument be administered to a sample of students before and after FLETC's training scenarios to establish the stress level for each scenario. The scenarios can then be classified by fact pattern and stress level to determine if the scenario matches the scenario designer's expectations. Scenarios not meeting expectations can then be revised.

Recommendation 2

The research team suggests that efforts be made to evaluate the number and amount of stress exposure training events needed to have an impact on reduction of errors and improvement of performance.

Recommendation 3

The study did not include any stress mitigation strategies as part of the investigation. There are techniques that could be introduced to assess their effectiveness and practicality. These strategies range from the simple (tactical breathing) to the more involved (desktop simulation). It is recommended that some of these strategies be investigated during future studies.

SECTION IV

The Impact of Feedback On Performance

4

The Impact of Feedback on Performance

Effective Training Feedback

When a student hears "out of role" and the training scenario ends, what takes place in the next few minutes between instructor and student will have a tremendous impact on the future capabilities of the student. Prompt and effective feedback is critical for capturing specific details related to decision making and performance in a scenario, and to build mental models in the future. In order to capitalize on this window of opportunity, the feedback should be positive, specific, and at an appropriate level, that will foster reflective thinking and improved performance. This section will present an overview of previous research on feedback techniques and share the results of a comparison between two feedback procedures used in this study.

Review of Feedback Research

Research has shown that properly structured and delivered feedback increases learning and skill proficiency, which is the ultimate mission of any training program. In 1984, a novel approach for the training of new physicians was conducted where medical problems were identified and treated through the use of open-ended questions (Pendleton, Schofield, Tate and Havelock, 1984). Although this was new in the medical field, it followed the classic process of Socratic questioning in order to produce a better result (a healthier and more self-aware patient). The primary objective was to make the consultation process "patient–centered" rather than "doctor–centered." In order for new physicians to acquire and develop their interviewing skills, a four step approach was used, that incorporated open-ended statements in order to determine the trainee's knowledge of the process, and to deliver appropriate guidance based upon the information provided by the trainee:

1. The student is asked to start by identifying his or her own strengths;

2. The trainer reinforces these and adds further strengths;

3. The student is asked to identify areas for improvement; and

4. The trainer reinforces these, adding further areas if necessary.

Paraskevas and Wickens (2003) describe the Socratic Method as a form of structured discourse using systematic questions, inductive thinking, and the formulization of general definitions with more emphasis on the process and less on content. A variation of Socratic Method is verbal probing. Verbal probing is an effective technique to gain an understanding of the cognitive processes employed during the activity (Ericsson and Simon, 1980). Using the process of "retrospective verbalization," students are asked to describe their actions immediately after the exercise. Beginning the feedback session with a non-evaluative question like, "From the time you began the scenario until we started this debriefing, describe what happened?" provides a means of probing without affecting the performance, as well as insight into the students' perspective of the scenario. The goal of this technique is not to pass judgment but to retrieve information. A key element of this step is to identify the result of the scenario.

Students appreciate feedback that is specific to their performance, and disregard nonspecific evaluative feedback (e.g. 'Good job') (Moorhead, Maguire, Thoo, 2004). Wood (2000) has provided some additional guidelines for this type of open-ended feedback:

1. Comments should be based on observable behavior and not on assumed intentions or interpretations.

2. Positive comments may be provided first to give the learner confidence.

3. Feedback should emphasize the sharing of information; both parties contribute.

4. Feedback should be given at an appropriate time and place.

5. Feedback should include specific, subjective data but not so detailed or broad as to overload the learner.

6. Feedback should deal with behaviors the learner can control and modify; it should deal with decisions and actions.

7. Learners should be asked to verify feedback.

8. Feedback requires preparation and the ability to tolerate discomfort and criticism.

The U.S. Navy has conducted extensive research on effective communication and the training process, and has developed a process that incorporates the use of open-ended sentences into a structured feedback process (Figure 4-1: TDT Feedback) for the training of groups or teams of individuals who work together (Smith-Jentsch, Zeisig, Acton, and McPherson, 1998). The process, known as Team Dimensional Training (TDT), provides instructors with structure to

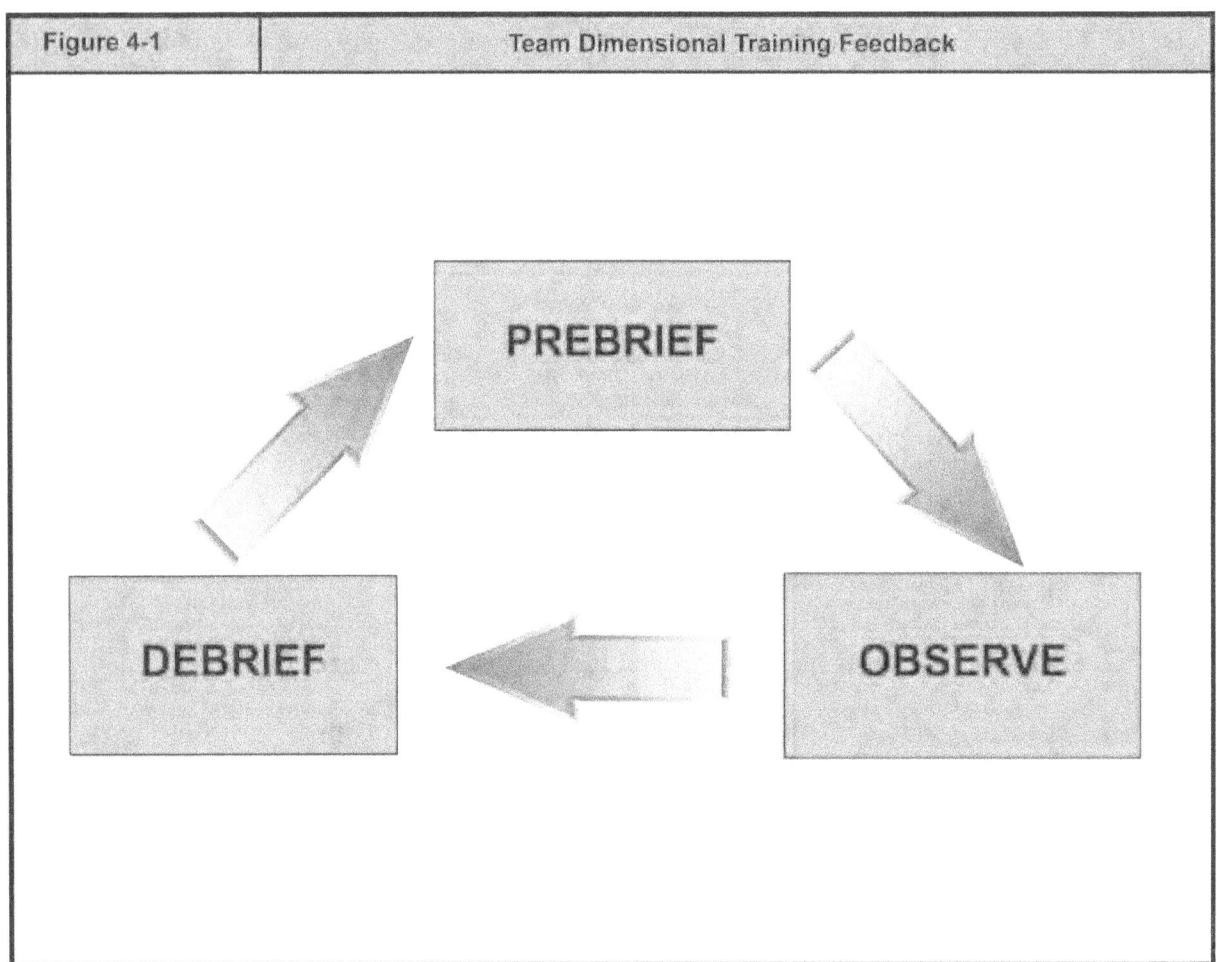

| Figure 4-1 | Team Dimensional Training Feedback |

(a) focus team members' attention during an exercise pre-brief, (b) observe the team's performance during an exercise, (c) diagnose the team's strengths and weaknesses after an exercise, and (d) guide the team through a self-critique of their performance. The self-critique phase uses open-ended statements and is almost entirely "student delivered" rather than "instructor delivered." This technique is designed to encourage student involvement and input, develop problem solving skills, provide each student with a feeling of ownership and contribution to the success of the team, and provide the instructor with a more complete picture of the students' knowledge and understanding of the performance. Again, the trainer has an opportunity to correct performance errors or clarify any misconceptions that are revealed in the session.

The success of these feedback models and the use of Socratic questioning guided the research team to focus on devising a six-step process that could potentially improve the training process at FLETC. This new procedure used open-ended statements which allowed the students to explain their actions and essentially do most of the talking. A second feedback procedure was then identified that involved the instructor doing most of the talking and was used as an alternative feedback procedure. The following paragraphs will describe the two feedback procedures used for this study in greater detail.

Instructor-Centered Feedback

Many current training programs follow an instructor-centered process where the instructor predominantly focuses on performance elements that were not done correctly. During the After Action Review (AAR) process, the instructor does the majority of speaking, correcting, and identification (hence the term, instructor-centered) of risks associated with the observed errors. The session is generally a synopsis of the observed performance errors along with specific skills that still require attention. This process works well when there is a limited amount of time.

Student-Centered Feedback

Following a review of literature on feedback, the research team developed a new feedback procedure that incorporated many of the practices recommended in the studies. For example, when open-ended statements are used, students immediately become active participants and the instructor will gain greater insight as to how students perceive their decisions and actions.

A feedback process that is student-centered also facilitates the use of higher mental processing described in Section 1 such as Application and Analysis or Moderate Transfer. The Student-Centered Feedback process provides repeated opportunities to ascertain what the student knows, correct misconceptions, and enhance the learning curve by reinforcing correct information and extinguishing incorrect information on multiple cognitive processing levels.

Another principle of feedback is that students tend to actively seek information to assess their progress and performance (Bandura, 1986). The characteristics of self-initiative and motivation are also critical to the learning process, for without any desire to learn new information or overcome a training deficiency, the student often fails or receives incomplete training. The internal motivation to learn and successfully perform a task is frequently described as self-efficacy. Machin (2002) reports that self-efficacy has a stronger influence on behavior than the student's knowledge and skills. Bandura (1997) takes the importance of self-efficacy a step further by stating it affects the decisions people make, how much effort they will exert, the length of perseverance when faced with a challenge, and their level of anxiety. Effective feedback during training enhances learning and each student's self-efficacy by increasing their confidence and competence to perform similar tasks in the future.

Student-Centered Feedback Model

The Student-Centered Feedback Model (Figure 4-2), illustrates the process developed by the research team during the study. In this process, instructors should begin by providing students with a pre-brief of the scenario that they are about to experience. The next step of the model requires instructors to observe the performance of the students during the scenario. To complete this portion of the process, instructors must be familiar with the data collection instruments and possess trained observation skills in order to document the performance of the students.

At the conclusion of the scenario, instructors should initiate the feedback session by asking students to identify their actions during the scenario. This is generally accomplished with the phrase, "From the time you began the scenario until we started this debriefing, describe what happened." Instructors can use other leading questions such as: "How did you become involved?", "What information did you collect prior to arriving on the scene?", and "What was your initial assessment of the situation?" The purpose of this step is to allow students to identify their actions, and for instructors to get a clearer understanding of how students perceive the situation and why they chose particular actions during the scenario.

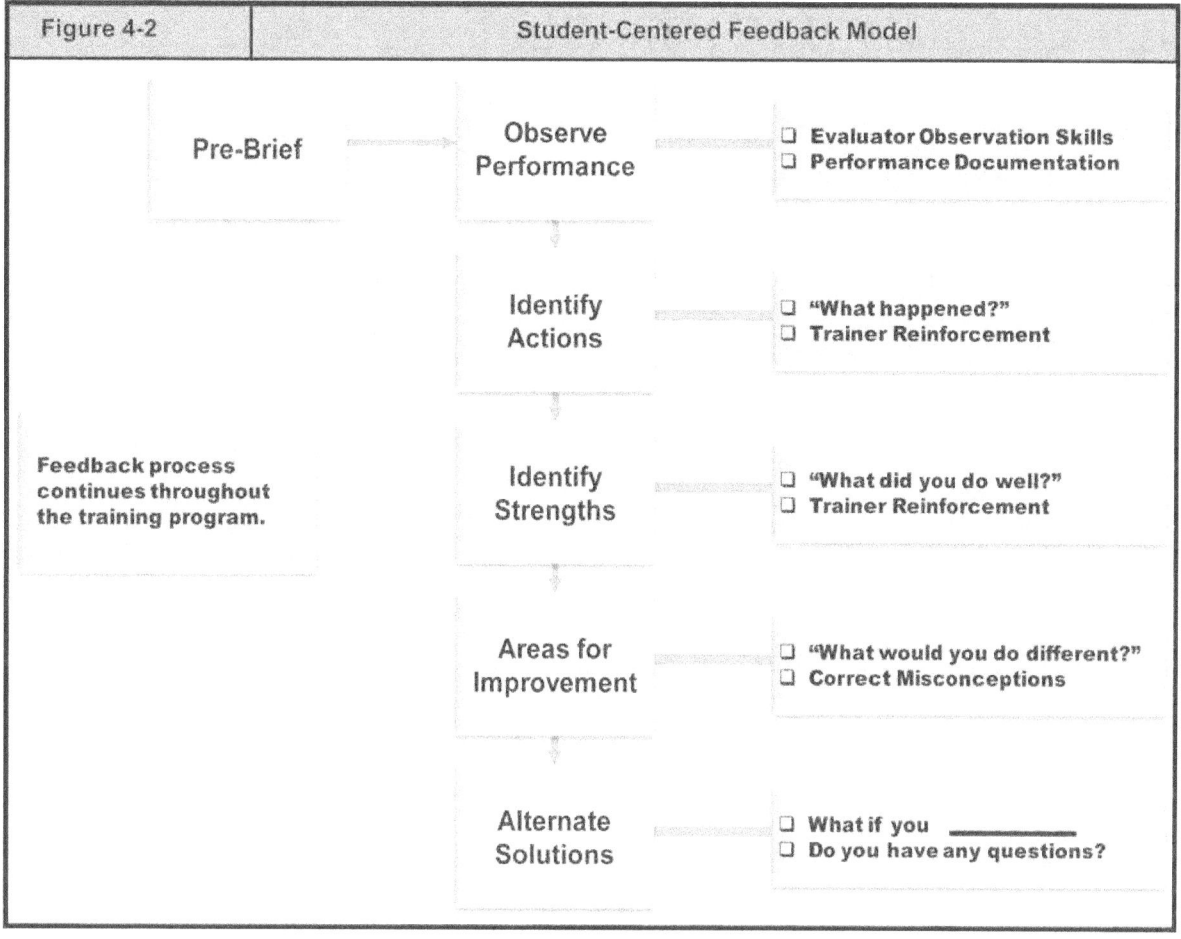

Pre-Brief

Feedback process continues throughout the training program.

Observe Performance — ❑ Evaluator Observation Skills ❑ Performance Documentation

Identify Actions — ❑ "What happened?" ❑ Trainer Reinforcement

Identify Strengths — ❑ "What did you do well?" ❑ Trainer Reinforcement

Areas for Improvement — ❑ "What would you do different?" ❑ Correct Misconceptions

Alternate Solutions — ❑ What if you _____ ❑ Do you have any questions?

Once students have identified what they did and why they did it, instructors should ask them to identify what were the strengths of their performance during the scenario, or in other words, what they did well. This accomplishes two objectives: it keeps the session on a positive note; and provides an opportunity to correct misconceptions (when students think something went well, when in fact it did not; or students state that they did poorly, when in fact they did reasonably well). This allows instructors to reinforce an effective thought process that correctly identifies and responds to a situation, and extinguishes incorrect thought processes or techniques that students may still have. These two steps enable the feedback session to be a positive and fruitful learning experience.

The next step of the model focuses on areas for improvement. Asking students a positive question like, "If you were to encounter this same event again, what would you do differently?" allows students to relive the experience and identify their own ways to improve their performance. This technique encourages students, develops problem solving skills, and provides instructors with a more complete picture of the students' knowledge and understanding of the performance. Again, instructors have an additional opportunity to correct misconceptions and provide additional feedback as necessary.

The next step in the process is to identify alternate solutions. Although this step provides another opportunity to reinforce critical thinking skills, it is just as important to avoid the pitfall of suggesting too many alternate solutions that will produce memory overload. The focus should be on one or two alternatives and allow students to do some problem solving and planning. This step also allows students a final opportunity to clarify any lingering uncertainties. At the conclusion of the alternate solutions step, instructors can focus on lessons learned and identify goals for improvement for the next scenario. The feedback process then repeats itself on the next activity, or retest on a similar scenario, to correct any identified performance issues.

Evaluation of Feedback Styles

All students encountered two lethal (Active Shooter and Armed Robbery) and two nonlethal (Trespasser and Attorney) force scenarios (Appendix 2: Research Scenarios). For consistency of delivery and comparison, the agreed upon characteristics of Instructor-Centered Feedback were: instructor over emphasizes basic skills with only one possible correct answer; instructor does virtually all of the talking during the feedback session; and the instructor's feedback is evaluative and critical, making the learning for the student very passive. During the feedback sessions, instructors were told to cut short a student's response if one was provided to explain/clarify their performance. While the instructor's demeanor during the Instructor-Centered Feedback session was authoritative and uncompromising, all comments were objective in nature based on specific performance errors observed during the scenario.

In contrast, the Student-Centered Feedback process emphasized critical thinking, problem solving, and creative solutions. The instructor's role during Student-Centered Feedback was to facilitate knowledge development. Feedback provided to the student was very descriptive and supportive in nature. While being supportive, the instructor provided corrective feedback to the student. Instructors did identify critical performance deficiencies but encouraged students to identify possible corrective actions. The primary communicator during Student-Centered

Feedback was the student. Encouraging student dialogue facilitated an active learning environment and enabled information sharing which further documented their knowledge, comprehension, application and analysis of law enforcement knowledge, skills and abilities. This form of feedback also enabled students to evaluate their performance as referenced to a performance standard, rather than compare their performance to other students or how the instructor would have performed.

First Day of the Study

After a briefing from an instructor, students began the Scenario One (Appendix 2: Response to Active Shooter). Immediately following the scenario, students were seated in a private interview room where, following the psychological tests, an instructor entered the room, and provided feedback to students regarding their performance on the preceding scenario. Prior to the start of the Scenario Two (Appendix 2: Non-Compliant Trespassing Protestor) of the evening, students returned to a private briefing room. Following Scenario Two, the student received feedback on their performance; and a second instructor conducted a situational awareness (SA) interview. During the SA interview, students were asked to recall details from the shoot scenario. Depending on the level of detail the student provided, the instructor would ask for additional information that would help to identify the extent of specific facts and details recalled by the student. The instructors typically used follow up questions like "How many people were present?", "How many threats?", and queries about elements that were not originally mentioned.

Second Day of the Study

The same protocol was used on day two as on day one; except that two new scenarios were used. Scenario Three focused on a Non-compliant Attorney, and Scenario Four was an Armed Robbery in Progress (Appendix 2: Research Scenarios). All four scenarios reflected similar fact patterns and required execution of the same law enforcement skills.

Scenario Performance Evaluation

The research team evaluated each student in the eight factors of the STAR scenario performance scale described in Section II. To ensure scoring fairness, the research team was never informed as to which feedback group a student was in. Each student's evaluation on the dimension criteria was established by consensus. The individual dimension score was obtained by determining the average score across the eight STAR items. The total survival score is determined by summing the weighted scores that comprise each subscale.

Results of Feedback Style

In order to determine if one feedback process had a measurable benefit over the other, students were randomly assigned into one of two groups: one receiving Instructor-Centered Feedback and the other receiving Student-Centered Feedback. Each student's performance was video-recorded during each scenario. Performance was defined as expected behaviors resulting from scenario cues/trigger events. The raw performance scores were converted into a percentage of total possible "desirable" responses. This score was used to reflect the performance level of each student in each scenario. Performance scores for all students were grouped by the type of feedback received and scenario. Figure 4-3: Performance Scores by Feedback Type and Scenario compares the two types of feedback during the scenarios. Even though student performance for the two lethal force scenarios and the two nonlethal force scenarios used the same evaluation instrument, the feedback scored higher in the Attorney scenario. All participants first participated in the Active Shooter scenario. Upon review of performance scores in this initial scenario, and comparing the scores by the two feedback procedures that the students were randomly assigned to, there was no measureable difference between the two groups. This similarity of performance levels allowed the initial scenario (Active Shooter) to serve as a baseline for measuring subsequent performance changes in the remaining three scenarios. For the Trespasser scenario, the Student-Centered Feedback scores ranged from a low of 18.33 to a high of 56.85, with a median score of 35.93. Instructor-Centered Feedback scores ranged from a low of 19.55 to a high of 51.38, with a median score of 29.80. For the Attorney scenario, the Student-Centered Feedback scores ranged from 20.42 to 74.79, with a median score of 29.61. The Instructor-Centered Feedback scores ranged from 19.58 to 68.82, with a median score of 34.79. For the Armed Robbery scenario, the Student-Centered Feedback scores ranged from 29.47 to 83.46, with a median score of 54.90. Instructor-Centered Feedback ranged from 29.58 to 84.74, with a lower median score of 42.80. Students receiving Student-Centered

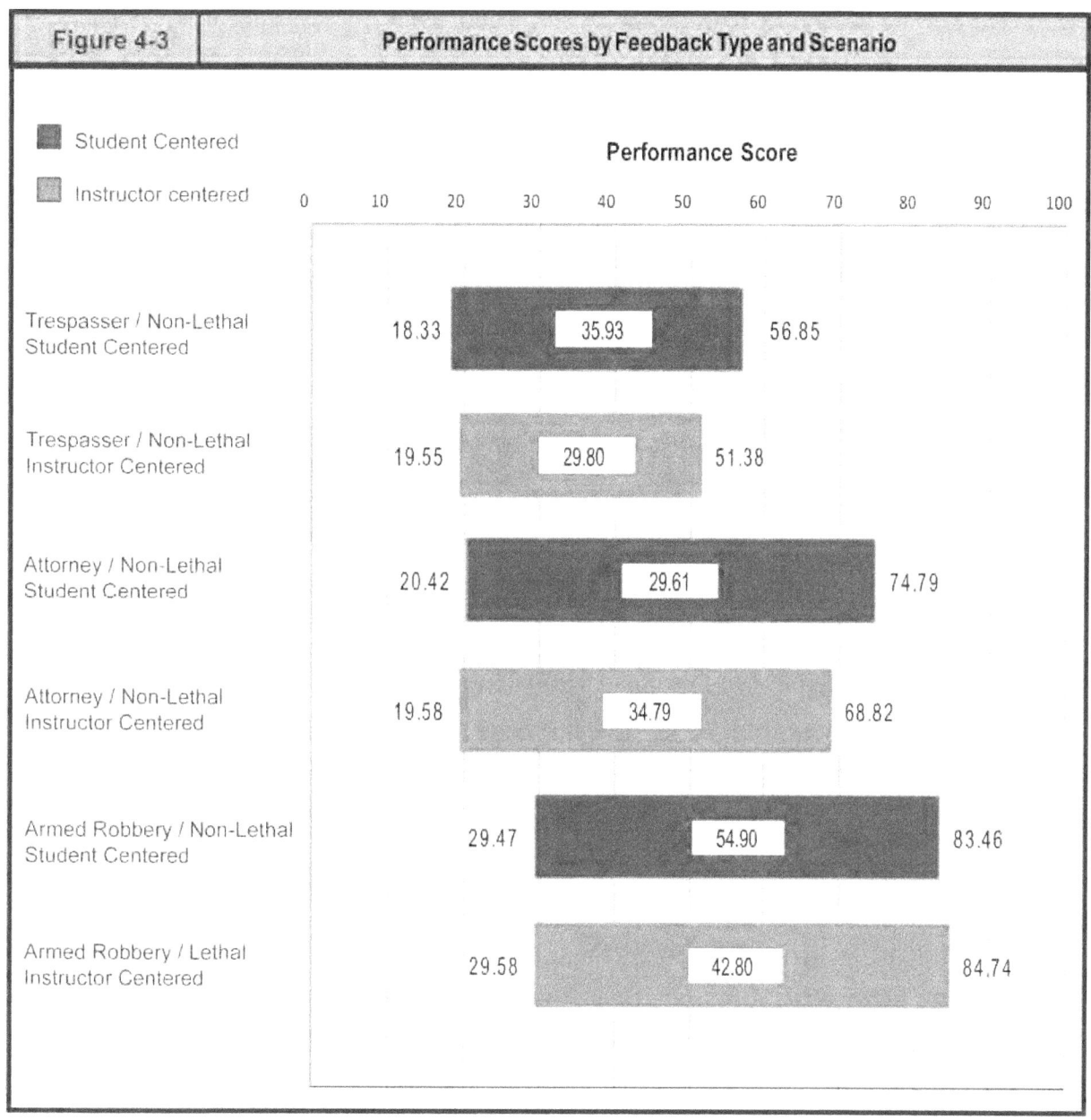

	Figure 4-3	Performance Scores by Feedback Type and Scenario

Performance Score

Student Centered
Instructor centered

Trespasser / Non-Lethal Student Centered: 18.33 — 35.93 — 56.85

Trespasser / Non-Lethal Instructor Centered: 19.55 — 29.80 — 51.38

Attorney / Non-Lethal Student Centered: 20.42 — 29.61 — 74.79

Attorney / Non-Lethal Instructor Centered: 19.58 — 34.79 — 68.82

Armed Robbery / Non-Lethal Student Centered: 29.47 — 54.90 — 83.46

Armed Robbery / Lethal Instructor Centered: 29.58 — 42.80 — 84.74

Feedback median scores averaged 4.4 points higher during the last three scenarios and scored 12.1 points higher (22 percent performance difference) during the last scenario (Armed Robbery).

During the final debriefing conducted at the end of the second day, students reflected on the scenarios and the feedback they received. Those students receiving Student-Centered Feedback commented that they enjoyed the feedback environment and felt that it provided insight into how to improve their performance. These students were excited about the scenarios and looked forward to each feedback session. The overall experience of students receiving Student-Centered Feedback was positive.

Those that received Instructor-Centered Feedback expressed frustration with the instructor providing feedback. The observed body language of the students in the Instructor-Centered Feedback group also indicated that they were uncomfortable during the session and rarely made any attempt to interact with the instructor. Although the students received detailed feedback that was specific to their performance, all indicated a preference for Student-Centered Feedback in the final assessment. Comments from students receiving Instructor-Centered Feedback indicated that the sessions were a negative experience.

All students received Student-Centered Feedback at the conclusion of the final scenario. Students who previously received Instructor-Centered Feedback overwhelming indicated that they preferred Student-Centered Feedback. Many students, from both groups, commented that the feedback they received during the research project was much more detailed and meaningful than what they received during training. The time allotment for feedback in this study was not as constrained as that of a class session, however, the benefits of Student-Centered Feedback should continue to be evaluated due to the favorable response by all students in the study.

Summary

Because learning is a two-way process, the knowledge, skills, abilities, and attitudes of the learner must be understood in order to optimize the transfer of information from instructor to student. Students desire to gain new knowledge and skills, and improve on existing levels of knowledge, skills, and abilities. Most students prefer to be challenged, compete against themselves and their peers, and satisfy their natural curiosity, training institutions should capitalize upon these traits. Training content should be designed to constantly challenge learners to maximize their learning experience. Student-Centered Feedback includes many of these factors in order to build upon their previous training and challenge each student. Half of the students in this study received feedback that was student-centered (students do the majority of talking to open-ended statements designed to build confidence, self-efficacy, and make the After Action Review [AAR] a generally positive experience). The structured questions allowed students to evaluate their scenario performance to identify what they would do differently if they could do the scenario again. Student-Centered Feedback was designed to challenge students by determining the current level of proficiency and improving upon it. This approach gives Student-Centered Feedback a tremendous advantage over Instructor-Centered Feedback – it takes students from where they are in terms of knowledge, skills, abilities, and experience, and builds upon that toward the desired goal.

The ability to provide feedback that is student-centered requires training and sufficient practice to acquire this unique skill. Initially, most instructors find it difficult and seemingly unnatural to allow the students to do the majority of the talking (by responding to open-ended statements). When students are given more time to talk, the instructor has a clearer picture of what the students' thought patterns were (or were not) during the training exercise. By allowing students to describe their situation awareness, threat awareness, proposed response, level of effectiveness, and future actions in a similar situation, a greater transfer of learning will take place as opposed to the instructor pointing out what was wrong and what was right.

Researchers reported that when feedback focuses on student performance rather than the outcome of the performance, it provides for greater skill development (Li, Solman, Lee, Purvis, and Chu, 2007). They also identified that the amount, content, frequency, precision, and type of feedback were the critical components of effective training feedback. Since feedback can be provided at different stages during the training process, the terms formative and summative feedback are routinely used. The term formative feedback describes information provided to the student for the sole purpose of improving future performance. In contrast, summative feedback is used in reference to a final performance or practical exercise that is graded to determine proficiency. Formative feedback requires information about a student's performance to be observed, documented, summarized, and fed back to the student, and generally offers the most promising way of improving student performance.

The research team documented the students' performance on checklists for each of the four scenarios. Performance was defined as expected behaviors resulting from scenario cues/trigger events. The study identified the effects of feedback in preparing students to select appropriate responses, integrating them into performance that remains resilient and effective in stressful, fast-moving confrontations. The Student-Centered Feedback model appears promising as a student training technique for highly dynamic training environments. Incorporation of proper tactics requires the ability to make effective decisions under stress. The ability to make decisions under threat conditions and implement these decisions to control the situation is a critical element for officer safety and survivability.

Recommendations

Recommendation 1

The findings of this report indicate that the STAR assessment model combined with Student-Centered Feedback are ideal tools to enhance training effectiveness and establish accurate mental models (memories) that are essential for effective law enforcement responses in dynamic, high stress encounters such as those presented in this study. The research suggests the adoption of the Student-Centered Feedback Model.

Recommendation 2

Observations during this comparative study identified inconsistencies in the delivery of feedback for law enforcement scenarios. To effectively implement the Student-Centered Feedback Model and prevent these inconsistencies the SSRP Team suggests that all instructors receive formal training on the delivery of Student-Centered Feedback.

Recommendation 3

The body of literature on Student-Centered Feedback, combined with comments from the participants, and general performance trends supports further research to determine if the effectiveness of feedback can be enhanced through video augmentation.

Appendix

Cited References

Artwohl, A. and W. Christensen. (1997). *Deadly Force Encounters*. Paladin Press, Boulder, Co.

Aven, T. (2006). On the precautionary principle, in the context of different perspectives on risk. *Risk Management: An International Journal*, 2006; 8:192-205.

Bandura, A. (1997). *Self-efficacy: The exercise of control*: WH Freeman New York.

Bandura, A. (1986). *Social foundations of thought and action: A social cognitive theory*: Prentice-Hall.

Bloom, B. S. (Ed.). (1956) *Taxonomy of Educational Objectives. Handbook I: Cognitive Domain*. NewYork: David McKay.

Bostain, J. (2006). Putting the Real in Reality-Based Training. *FLETC Journal, 4*(1), 14-16.

Cannon-Bowers, J. A., Salas, E., and Converse, S. (2001) Shared Mental Models in Expert Team Decision Making. in R. J. Sternberg and E. L. Grigorenko (Eds.) *Environmental Effects on Cognitive Abilities*. (pp. 221-246) London: Psychology Press..

Clark, Ruth C. (2008). Building Expertise: cognitive methods for training and performance improvement: John Wiley and Sons.

Driskell, J. E., and Johnston, J. H. (1998). Stress exposure training. *Making decisions under stress: Implications for individual and team training*, 191-217.

Driskell, J. E., Salas, E., Johnston, J. H., and Wollert, T. N. (2008). Stress exposure training: An event-based approach. *Performance under stress*, 271-286.

Endsley, M. R., Bolte, B., and Jones, D. G. (200**3).** Designing for Situation Awareness: An approach to human-centered design. London: Taylor and Francis.

Endsley, M.R., and Robertson, M.M. (2000). Training for situation awareness in individuals and teams. In M. R. Endsley and D. J. Garland (Eds.), *Situation awareness analysis and measurement*. Mahwah, NJ: LEA.

Ericsson, K. A., and Simon, H. A. (1980). Verbal reports as data. *Psychological Review, 87*(3), 215-251.

Federal Bureau of Investigation. (2006). *Violent Encounters*. Washington D.C.: U.S. Department of Justice.

Federal Bureau of Investigation. (1997). *FBI Uniform Crime Report*. Retrieved March 13, 2007, from http://www.fbi.gov/ucr/killed/97killed.pdf.

Federal Law Enforcement Training Center. (2004). *Survival scores research project*. Glynco, GA: Author.

Fowlkes, J. E., Dwyer, D., Oser, R. L., and Salas, E. (1998) Event based approach to training (EBAT). *The International Journal of Aviation Psychology, 8 (3)*, 209-221.

Jentsch, F., and Cannon-Bowers, A. (1998). Evidence for the validity of PC-based simulations in studying aircrew communication. *International Journal of Aviation Psychology 8*, 243–260.

Johnston, J. H., and Cannon-Bowers, J. A. (1996). Training for stress exposure. *Stress and human performance (A 97-27090 06-53), Mahwah, NJ, Lawrence Erlbaum Associates, Publishers, 1996*, 223-256.

Klein, G. (2004). *The power of intuition: How to use your gut feelings to make better decisions at work*: Currency.

Li, W., Solmon, M. A., Lee, A. M., Purvis, G., and Chu, H. (2007). Examining the relationships between students' implicit theories of ability, goal orientations and the preferred type of augmented feedback. *Journal of Sport Behavior, 30*(3), 280-291.

Machin, M. A. (2002). Planning, managing, and optimizing transfer of training. In K. Kraiger (Ed.), *Creating, implementing, and managing effective training and development: State-of-the-art lessons for practice*. San Francisco: Jossey-Bass.

Meichenbaum, D. (2003). Stress inoculation training: A preventative and treatment approach. *Principles and practice of stress management, 3*, 497-518.

Murray, K. R. (2004). *Training at the Speed of Life* (Vol. 1). Gotha: Armiger Publications.

Moorhead, R., Maguire, P., and Thoo, S. L. (2004). Giving feedback to learners in the practice. *Australian Family Physician, 33*(9), 691 - 694.

NLEOMF. (2011). *Law Enforcement Fatalities Spike Dangerously in 2010*. [Electronic Version]. Memorial News, 1-4, retrieved 1/11/2011.

Paraskevas, A., and Wickens, E. (2003). Andragogy and the socratic method: The adult learner perspective. *Journal of Hospitality, Leisure, Sport and Tourism Education, 2*(2), 4–14.

Pendleton D, Schofield, T., Tate P., and Havelock P. (1984). *The consultation: An approach to learning and teaching.* Oxford: Oxford University Press.

Plehn, M. (2000). Control warfare: Inside the OODA loop. *Unpublished Master's Thesis, Air University, School of Advanced Airpower Studies, Maxwell AFB, AL.*

Prince, M. and R. Felder. (2007). The many faces of inductive teaching and learning. Journal of College Science Teaching, 36(5), 14-20.

Ravizza, K. (2007). *Controlling Emotions: How to Feel Comfortable When You Are Uncomfortable* Paper presented at the 2007 Peaksports Mental Training Boot Camp Orlando, FL 32819.

Ross, D. L. (2008, Feb 01 and 05). *Lessons learned from lethal force encounters* (part 1 and 2). Retrieved from http://www.policeone.com/legal/articles/1658333-Lessons-learned-from-lethal-force-encounters/

Schechtman, G. M. (1996). *Manipulating the ooda loop: The overlooked role of information resource management in information warfare.* Air Force Institute of Technology.

Schmidt, R. A., and Wrisberg, C. A. (2008). *Motor learning and performance: a situation-based learning approach*: Human Kinetics Publishers.

Smith-Jentsch, K. A., Zeisig, R. L., Acton, B., and Mcpherson, J. A. (1998). Team dimensional training: A strategy for guided team self-correction. *Making decisions under stress: Implications for individual and team training*, 271-297.

Spielberger, C. D., and Reheiser, E. C. (2004). Measuring anxiety, anger, depression, and curiosity as emotional states and personality traits with the STAI, STAXI, and STPI. H. M. Herson, and D.L. Segal (Ed.), *Comprehensive Handbook of Psychological Assessment: Personality assessment, 1972*, (Vol. 2, pp. 70-86). Hoboken: John Wiley and Sons, Inc.

Spielberger C.D., Ritterland, L. M., Sydeman, S. J., Reheiser E. C., and Unger K. K. (1995). Assessment of Emotional States and Personality Traits: Measuring Psychological Vital Signs. In J. N. Butcher (Ed.), *Clinical Personality Assessment: Practical Approaches* (pp. 42-58). New York: Oxford University Press.

Spielberger, C. D. (1979). Preliminary Manual for the State-Trait Personality Inventory (STPI). Unpublished Scoring guide. University of South Florida.

Spielberger, C. D., and Reheiser, E. C. (2009). Assessment of Emotions: Anxiety, Anger, Depression, and Curiosity. *Applied Psychology: Health and Well-Being, 1*(3), 271-302.

Wood, B. P. (2000). A key feature of medical training many diverse methods of instruction are used throughout a training experience, but the most available and influential method of learning probably is feedback. *RADIOLOGY-OAK BROOK IL-, 215*(1), 17-21.

www.ingramcontent.com/pod-product-compliance
Lightning Source LLC
Chambersburg PA
CBHW081846280526
45789CB00007B/2581